Dangerous Families

Peter Dale, Murray Davies,
Tony Morrison, and Jim Waters

Dangerous Families

Assessment and treatment of child abuse

London and New York

First published in 1986 by
Tavistock Publications Ltd

Reprinted 1987

Reprinted 1989 and 1992 by Routledge
11 New Fetter Lane, London EC4P 4EE
29 West 35th Street, New York, NY 10001

Phototypeset by MC Typeset, Chatham, Kent
Printed and bound in Great Britain by
Richard Clay Ltd, Bungay, Suffolk

British Library Cataloguing in Publication Data

Dangerous families: assessment and treatment of child abuse.
  1. Child abuse—Great Britain—
  Prevention
  I. Dale, Peter, 1946-
  362.7'044   HV751.A6

Library of Congress Cataloging in Publication Data

Dangerous families.
  Bibliography: p.
  Includes index.
  1. Child abuse—Great Britain.   2. Child abuse—Great Britain—Prevention.
  3. Family social work—Great Britain.   I. Dale, Peter. [DNLM:
  1. Child Abuse.   2. Family.   3. Family Therapy. WA 320 D182]
  HV6626.5.D36   1986   362.7'044   86-6038

ISBN 0-415-03696-8

Contents

Acknowledgements

The team owes its existence to John Pickett (Principal Social Work Manager, NSPCC) and Lyndon Price (former Director of Rochdale Social Services Department), who were responsible for successfully negotiating the original financial provision. The continuing support of Gordon Littlemore (Director of Rochdale Social Services Department) and Deryk Mead (Deputy Director of Rochdale Social Services Department) has been invaluable.

We would like to record our appreciation to all of the practitioners of each relevant profession within the borough of Rochdale, in particular to the social workers and managers of Rochdale Social Services Department, and to the health visitors and their managers of Rochdale Area Health Authority. Their constant contact and involvement with the team provided indispensable stimulation for the work described in this book to develop.

From within the NSPCC we are grateful for the encouragement of senior management, particularly that of the Director, Dr Alan Gilmour, CBE, and Mr John Low, OBE, Secretary, who skilfully navigated the progress of the book through some hidden obstacles. Our appreciation is also expressed to Mr Fred Hedley, Legal Secretary, and Mr Alan Bedford, Training Manager, for their helpful comments on the manuscript. In addition, Christine Smakowska, Annette Briggs, and all of the staff in the NSPCC Headley Library have consistently assisted us by their cheerful ability to obtain the most obscure of references.

At a local level, the team could not have succeeded without the support of the Chairman of the local NSPCC Branch Committee, Mr Jack Howarth. Within the team, we have been unusually fortunate in the quality of our secretarial and administrative staff.

Pauline Wilson (Team Administrator), Julie Bowmer (Team Secretary), Elaine Halliwell, Carole Smith, and Liz Timmons have sustained us efficiently whilst consistently teasing us for our various impossible idiosyncrasies.

Work began in 1980 with the integration of the established local NSPCC Inspector, Wilf Roberts, into the new team. The authors remain indebted to Wilf for his patience, understanding, and calmness, as he quietly and consistently played a major role in the development of the team by sharing his unique depth of understanding, experience, skills, and wisdom.

Finally, our own families have suffered long periods of 'author abuse', especially our children: Nathan, Rory, and Rosanna Dale; Corin and Sorcha Davies; Sarah and Stevie Waters; and Christopher Morrison. To them, and to Sue, Val, Chris, and Jacqui, our apologies.

Peter Dale
December 1985

Preface

This book is aimed at practitioners dealing with child-abusing families in a range of clinical and statutory settings. It provides a clear model for the assessment and treatment of such families, and encourages the use of a variety of modern psychotherapeutic techniques from the creative base of a therapeutic team.

A major theme of the book is the processes by which the range of social agencies can play a pathological role by unintentionally contributing to and maintaining child-abusing dynamics in families. As well as describing methods of intervention to protect children and promote positive change in dangerous families, the book also addresses the phenomenon of dangerous professionals. By outlining the necessity for therapeutic intervention in the professional systems – as well as the family system – the book presents a major change of view in the understanding, management, and treatment of child abuse.

It is hoped that the book will be of direct practical use to professionals of all disciplines, and that the exposure of the work of our team in this way will enable other practitioners to identify overtly processes in families, agencies, and their work, which had previously operated covertly to the detriment of good professional practice.

The major hope of the authors is that practitioners in mainstream statutory settings – where the vast majority of the unrecognized and largely unrewarding grind of child-protective social work occurs – will be encouraged to form themselves into therapeutic teams, and experience and enjoy the increased professional skill and effectiveness which result.

In attempting to do so, resistance from certain managerial levels within each agency may be predicted: 'Why does it take three of you? It only took one in my day.' It is hoped that the structure of work presented throughout the book will give confidence to managers to allow degrees of change, as well as providing some tactics by which practitioners may provoke this change. In doing so, it may be helpful to bear the two important principles of our team in mind:

For families: Is the child safe? – *Protection before therapy.*
For practitioners and teams: *Look after yourselves.*

CHAPTER 1

The professional context of child abuse

Development of services

It is almost traditional to begin accounts of the development of child abuse recognition with a mention of the scandal of Mary Ellen in New York in 1874. Mary Ellen suffered serious ill-treatment at the hands of her adoptive parents who had insisted that it was their parental right to treat her as they wished. Laws existed to protect animals from ill-treatment, but not children; so legal action was brought on behalf of the child as 'a member of the animal kingdom'. The case was found proved and she was granted protection. The foundation of the New York Society for the Prevention of Cruelty to Children followed; this was the inspiration behind the British National Society for the Prevention of Cruelty to Children (NSPCC), founded in 1884.

In the following century there was a rapid development of child care legislation which reflected the constant tension between the need to protect children and the need to respect parental rights.

Public alarm about individual cases has often provided an impetus for urgent changes in legislation and services. The death of Dennis O'Neill, a war evacuee murdered by his foster parents, was an important influence behind the formulation of the Children Act, 1948, and the establishment in that year of the local authority Children's Departments.

In a later era, the death of Maria Colwell in 1973 had enormous implications for the organization and management of child care services. Maria's death also began another swing away from the 'rights' of natural parents, decreasing the emphasis on the importance of the 'blood tie' in decision-making about children in care. As a consequence, the Children Act, 1975, was intended to strengthen significantly the position of foster parents and other substitute care-takers, including prospective adoptive parents.

The decade of the 1970s was a traumatic one for child care services in Britain. There were several major structural reorganizations of agencies; local government boundary changes; a succession of critical public inquiries into the role of agencies in cases where children had been killed by their parents; all in the context of a new era of increasing constraint on public expenditure.

The creation of the social services departments in 1971 brought under the same administration the services for children, the mentally ill, and the elderly which had previously been provided by separate agencies. This was an overdue rationalization of family services (previously it was not unknown for social workers from several different departments to be visiting the same family), but it also brought some new bureaucratic difficulties. Many experienced practitioners were tempted into the new management posts on offer, only to find themselves without management skills in strange and unfamiliar territory.

Into the vacuum left by the newly created managerial class arrived a new breed of social workers, either untrained or straight from university, inexperienced and generic. Most social services departments in the early 1970s had taken the recommendations of the Seebohm report (which had led to the creation of the generic departments) too literally, and expected all workers to become competent in all aspects of social work, rather than expecting the goal of genericism to exist within the team as a whole. In consequence specialist skills were either lost or never developed during this period, at the expense of the professionalism of the work undertaken, and the confidence of other professionals.

A determined bid for training by social services departments throughout the 1970s gradually remedied this position, and many local authorities invested heavily in obtaining fully qualified fieldwork staff; and saw this repaid in terms of a more effective and respected service. Social work morale, however, continued to be undermined by developments throughout the decade and into the 1980s. From Maria Colwell onwards, there was a steady stream of inquiries into cases of fatal child abuse, and considerable material became available for what became a sustained and at times sensational attack on professional groups by a large part of the media. The behaviour and reporting of certain newspapers were contemptible.

The public image of social work suffered intense negative exposure, indeed rapid tarnishing. The loss of professional confidence (in the face of the joke of the time – 'save a child, kill a social worker') resulted in workers and their agencies adopting a self-protective approach. Work became cautious to the point of being dismal, unfocused, and over-sustained; frequency of visiting assumed greater importance than the content of the visit itself.

It would be wrong, however, to suggest that the effect of the public inquiries was totally negative. Most of them demonstrated that in addition to the graphically revealed problems of inter-agency communication and co-operation, there was no reliable model or knowledge base available from which decision-making and treatment plans could stem. The inquiries have had a fundamental effect on the creation of structures for the co-ordination of the services of the different agencies with a role in the protection of children. Area review committees comprising the heads of these agencies are required to formulate local guidelines for the management of all identified child abuse cases in their areas. Case-conference systems and child abuse registers exist locally throughout the country to enable more efficient monitoring of child abusing families.

Social workers and other professionals often find such proce-dures irritating and frustrating, and complain about further 'bureaucratization' of their professional duties. Often the profes-sionals making such complaints are not aware of the significant *preventive* role that clearly defined and administered procedures relating to child abuse are shown to have. NSPCC research has consistently demonstrated that areas of the country with tight management procedures show a significant drop in the incidence of *serious* child abuse.

Organization of services

Local authority social work in Britain appears to be afflicted by the compulsive need of senior management and local politicians to reorganize continually the structures of the departments and teams from which services are delivered. Sometimes it appears that this is an impulsive response to a temporary ideological or political whim. The Barclay report added further fuel to the existing debate between proponents of 'specialist' client-group teams, and advocates of 'patch' locally based teams. (Specialist teams focus on client-groups – e.g. children or the mentally ill – while 'patch' teams deal with all types of cases within their small geographical area.)

There is currently a tremendous variation in the way social services are organized by local authorities in Britain. Some departments are decentralizing rapidly, whilst near neighbours are reorganizing into specialist teams. Some departments are reversing relatively recent changes which staff have still not understood, and others seem to be reorganizing with no clear policy at all. Managers need to be more aware that such constant change breeds uncertainty and frustration among staff, and that poor morale amongst child protective social workers very quickly may become counter-productive and ultimately dangerous.

The services of the NSPCC are by no means unaffected by radical changes stemming from developments in professional practice and reorganization of other agency structures. The NSPCC as a charity heavily dependent on public support and subscription has needed to be responsive and innovative throughout its hundred-year history in developing new services for the protection of children.

A major change occurred in the 1970s with the development of a number of Special Units which provided intensive treatment facilities for identified abusing families. Many of the Special Units also provided management services in respect of the local child abuse procedures. This involved convening, chairing, and taking minutes at case-conferences; providing a consultation service to other professionals; and holding and maintaining the child abuse register. The work of the Special Units was a complete contrast to traditional NSPCC social work (an individual inspector, often covering a very large area, responding to calls from the public about children thought to be at risk). The inspector's role was essentially a preventive one, with much emphasis placed on the organization of material support for families.

In any organization change and development in practices creates feelings of uncertainty in staff with many years' experience of established methods. The NSPCC is no exception. The 1984

'Centenary Charter' announced the society's intention to reorganize its inspectors and the social workers in the fourteen Special Units into sixty Child Protection Teams. Each team would have a specifically locally negotiated remit with the social services and health agencies in the area; thus teams with different functions and styles would emerge to meet local needs. The NSPCC would continue to ensure that a protective response is made to reports it receives of children at risk on a country-wide, twenty-four-hour basis. The Rochdale Special Unit officially became the first of the new Child Protection Teams on 1 July, 1984.

Therapeutic models

Care and control

The concepts of care and control have always been uneasy partners within many fields of therapeutic activity. The professions of social work, psychiatry, and education constantly face dilemmas provoked by simultaneous pressures to provide care *and* control for their clients, patients, and pupils. Models of 'pure' care or control can be characterized, but it is increasingly recognized that in many therapeutic areas it can be counter-productive to hold to a model which attempts to separate care from control. The concepts have become artificially and misleadingly polarized. In fact care and control are essentially part of the same process, as any parent of a young child will be aware: each aspect is necessary for the effective application of the other.

The evolution of treatment models has been characterized by Parton (1979) as involving the interplay of three intellectual and professional groupings: a medical model, a legal model, and a social-welfare model. The tension between issues of care and control, and of rights against responsibilities, runs through the development of each model.

The medical model assumed an ascendancy in the 1960s following from the work of Henry Kempe and his associates. Kempe drew public and professional attention to the phenomenon of child abuse in an almost evangelical way, and developed a therapeutic programme which rapidly became influential throughout the US and Britain. Therapy was based on a strictly psychoanalytic understanding of the dynamics of child abuse. The act of abuse was seen as involving a 'transference psychosis', graphically described by Steele and Pollock (1968):

> 'the events begin with the parent's identification of the infant for whom he is caring as a need gratifying object equivalent to a parent who will replace the lacks in the abusing parent's own being-parented experience. Since the parent's past tells him that the ones to whom he looked for love were also the ones who attacked him, the infant is also perceived as a critical parent figure. . . . The perception of being criticized stirs up the parent's feelings of being inferior. It also increases the frustration of his need for love, and anger mounts. At this time there seems to be a strong sense of guilt, a feeling of helplessness and panic becomes overwhelming, and the haziness is most marked. Suddenly a shift in identification occurs. The superego identification with the parent's own punitive parent takes over. The infant is perceived as the parent's own bad childhood self. The built up aggression is redirected outwardly and the infant is hit with full superego approval.'

The origins of these dynamics were seen as being firmly rooted in early childhood experiences of the parents' specifically damaging relationships with their own parents. As children they lacked the satisfactions of being dependent on a reliable mother-figure, and experienced a sense of intense and pervasive demands from their parents.

Kempe's treatment model followed the American casework tradition epitomized by Reiner and Kaufman (1959). The process involved the development of a long-term nurturing relationship geared towards the satisfaction of unmet dependency needs, with the ultimate aim of providing re-parenting for the parents. The empathy and availability of the worker were seen as the essential elements; these would be expressed by demonstrations of acceptance of and 'care' for the parents as part of the crucial attempt to overcome the barrier of their basic mistrust.

It was considered essential to separate between different workers the function of taking any necessary (controlling) legal action to protect the child, and the task of the primary worker who would provide the therapeutic nurturing. Similarly, it was considered necessary to provide separate workers for each parent as it was felt that the levels of egocentricity were such that parents would be unable to tolerate sharing a therapist.

The British context

In Britain the therapeutic model pioneered by Kempe was utilized by the NSPCC Battered Child Research Department (Denver House) which was established in London under the personal influence of Kempe in 1968. The team had a specific research and treatment remit, and worked in almost ideal circumstances. The Denver House team adopted a firm stance in respect of the criminal process and the separation of care and controlling functions:

> 'since our main emphasis was to be on treatment and rehabilitation, we felt that we would prefer that they [the police] were not involved with our families, as we did not believe that they had a therapeutic role to play in battered baby cases. Our intention was to avoid any direct interrogation about the circumstances of an injury, and we were anxious that our parents should avoid this experience from others.'
>
> (Baher *et al.* 1976: 106)

The team expressed concern about the disadvantages of removing children from abusing families, including the risk of seriously alienating parents by taking legal action. However, there was an awareness that the child's physical safety should be the main consideration. The American model of separation of legal and therapeutic tasks was followed, and the local authority children's departments became responsible (somewhat unwillingly) for any necessary court proceedings, leaving the Denver House workers free to concentrate on forming a purely 'therapeutic' relationship with the parents.

In practice, the split between the 'good' and 'bad' workers did not work out as envisaged. The 'bad' social workers were unenthusiastic about their role, and on several occasions were less inclined towards removal of the child than the 'good' worker. On occasions, plans were sabotaged. Treatment would last between eighteen months and three years:

> 'the therapeutic relationship was intended to provide for some

of the parents' unmet dependency needs. In fostering the
parents' emotional development, it was hoped that their
capacity to care for the child would improve . . . casework
was seen as an essentially long-term restitutive process in
which we would imaginatively nurture the deprived areas of
the personality.'   (Baher *et al*. 1976: 134)

The Denver House team acknowledged their lack of success in
involving fathers in the therapeutic programme; most fathers were
felt to remain mistrusting throughout the intervention. A few
fathers actively sought to sabotage the therapeutic help accepted
by their wives. Such behaviour was entirely understandable when
viewed from a family systems perspective.

The overall effect of the Denver House team was to encourage
the NSPCC to consider a further development. This was the
establishment of a series of Special Units, the first of which was set
up in Manchester in 1973. The Manchester Special Unit pioneered
the model which was adopted by most later units (including
Rochdale) of combining treatment, management, and consultation functions.

For the original Manchester team, the model for understanding
the dynamics of abuse was predominantly based on the work of
Kempe, although, as with the Denver House team, set within a
recognition of the influence of social deprivation. Treatment
followed the nurturing approach, although with some important
amendments. The Manchester team did not avoid a detailed focus
on the actual event of abuse, but considered it and its precipitating
cause to be a crucial assessment area. The process of separating
legal and therapeutic functions among different workers was
abandoned, and in over half of their cases the unit worker
instigated legal proceedings to protect the child.

The major therapeutic advance of the Manchester unit was in
looking to co-ordinate caring *and* controlling functions. Thus there
were two major goals: '(a) We encourage a large element of
dependency on the worker, who offers understanding, empathy,
help, support, reliability, and dependability. . . . (b) We impose
some degree of control on a family situation which has clearly
broken down in a massive and fundamental way' (Pickett and
Maton 1977: 56–80).

Like the Denver House team, the Manchester team found that

the outcome of the treatment they provided was disadvantaged by their failure to engage fathers in the therapeutic process. The team's conclusions were familiar:

> 'Where we are able to work with some effect with one partner, a disparity grows between husband and wife and we are not able to demonstrate effective intervention in those families fraught with marital disharmony . . . we are not able to demonstrate in many cases that the overall qualitative life experiences of the children or the quality of their parenting improves.'
>
> (Pickett and Maton 1977)

Understanding poor results

The work of the Denver House team and the original Manchester Special Unit represented a highly professional application of a therapeutic model which in retrospect can be seen to have serious theoretical and practical flaws. A major feature of the nurturing model is the emphasis on intra-psychic and social factors, particularly emotional and social deprivation, as determining family relationships, including the relationship of abuse. History is seen to dominate, therapy is restitutive, and parental maturation is the goal. Workers adopting this approach tended to acknowledge the powerlessness of the parents to influence their own lives, and would accept the responsibility on their behalf for promoting change. The emphasis was on acceptance and provision, whilst the need for control and the establishment of limits to behaviour was undervalued.

The re-parenting model as applied in such ways to child abuse fails as the theoretically essential can never be achieved in reality – the worker can never be an effective parent to the client. The model of acceptance (particularly the Denver House practice of avoiding focusing on the actual injury) represented a dangerously false conception of good parenting. A confusion arose as to who the client was: the parent with the disastrous history of emotional deprivation? or the child who is in need of protection? What happens when the emotional needs of the parent and the child are incompatible? If the primary focus is on forming an accepting and nurturing relationship with the abusing parent, where does that leave the child?

In the following description of the development of the 'modern psychotherapies' it will be seen that the major element of change stems from the importance of individuals and families themselves taking responsibility for their lives. The role of the therapist becomes less to do with changing others, than to do with providing the context for people to make their own changes.

It was in this context of radical change in therapeutic attitudes, together with a decline in available resources, that throughout the 1970s the original enthusiasm about re-parenting models for child-abusing families rapidly diminished. If the process had a questionable value when applied by well-resourced and experienced specialist teams, where did that leave the workers in a typical over-stretched generic social services department? Social work with child-abusing families largely moved into a phase of anxious surveillance of families, with practitioners only noting rather than influencing events, whilst also attempting to implement uncoordinated, highly pragmatic 'solutions' to presenting problems without the advantage of reference to an effective knowledge or practice base. In the climate of the public inquiries it became essential for agencies and workers to protect themselves as part of the task of attempting to protect children. Social work became dismal, cautious, and increasingly procedurally regulated.

One effect of the publicity surrounding the Maria Colwell inquiry was an enormous increase in the following years in the use of place of safety orders, and other types of legal proceedings to remove children from homes where they were considered to be at serious risk. Unfortunately, once the children were in care there was little consistency as to how decisions about their future should be taken. Care orders often became ends in themselves, as if they would magically produce change in the functioning of the family. Children drifted in care for long periods, often through multiple placements, often becoming significantly emotionally damaged in the process.

When such children were returned home, it was often on the basis of the provision of maximum 'supplemental services', for example full-time day nursery placements and peripatetic family aides. The idea was to contribute to children's safety by minimizing the amount of time they spent in the care of their parents. Such supplemental services were also used, often covertly, to add to the 'surveillance' of the child back at home within the family. This era of social work ignored a warning from the previous decade: 'Findings suggest that multiplicity of workers and over-frequent observation of battering families can increase family stress, and a type of supervision of a family which is limited to an anxious watchfulness without specific treatment goals is not in the child's interest' (Skinner and Castle 1969: 20).

Fourteen years later, the same point was made again, in characteristically more assertive fashion by Salvador Minuchin. Describing the operation of the agencies involved with Maria Colwell and her family, he stated: 'Surveillance killed Maria' (Minuchin 1983). The uncomfortable fact that 'solutions' can themselves become a dangerous part of the child-abuse problem is commented on throughout this book.

Modern psychotherapies

It is to be expected that as one therapeutic era declines, new ideas arise to fill the space. In total contrast to the mood of child abuse treatment in the late 1970s, this period also witnessed intense excitement about the upsurge and potential of several modern psychotherapies. The decade saw an immense output of theoretical and therapeutic energy expended as 'new' methods were employed to tackle old problems. Family therapy, one of the most prominent of the emerging disciplines, began to establish a reputation and effectiveness primarily in psychiatric and child-guidance settings.

Social workers in such settings were eager to participate in and contribute to a powerful therapeutic approach which did not in itself function according to traditional medical views of status or omnipotence. Gradually, such enthusiasm filtered across into social work agencies, and by the end of the decade in many areas there were established 'Family Therapy Support Groups' which brought together a range of enthusiasts from different agencies. Many support groups operated overtly to encourage family therapy thinking and practice, and as a forum for finding co-therapists and consultation. Many also had a covert function as pressure groups for change within agencies, and often as a consequence were viewed with suspicion by management.

The development of family therapy

Family therapy has become a growth industry over the last twenty years. Its development has involved an evolutionary process of mutual influence between several distinct theoretical models. There is no single 'family therapy', but a collection of 'family therapies', with a good deal of stimulation – and rivalry – between the adherents of different schools.

For the sake of simplicity in a brief overview, three major models of influence in current family therapy can be identified: historical, structural, and strategic. This is not to say that the models are completely distinct, nor that the principles of one are not relevant to another. Certain concepts are shared to some extent in each of the family therapy models.

Shared concepts

Importance of process *versus* content

Processes are sequential patterns of behaviour which occur normally and spontaneously in any social group, and which constitute rules and regulations of behaviour which are often unrecognized and unacknowledged. In any group, but specifically in families, the sequences of speech and behaviour possess power and meaning quite separate from the content of what is said or done. Often this is most significant with regard to *roles* which family members adopt.

Family therapists will observe carefully the process of roles in families. There may be a child who becomes ill or badly behaved to *distract* attention away from something the family as a whole experiences as discomforting – perhaps marital disharmony. There may be a parent or elder child who has the role of *rescuer* – who steps into every disagreement or conflict offering 'solutions', and thus prevents the parties involved from working out their own conciliation. There may be a *disagreer* who will always find ways in which such 'solutions' will not work. It is likely in such situations that the 'rescuer' and the 'disagreer' will become locked into a repetitive process of conflict and argument. They may squabble about the most appropriate ways to 'help' a passive *victim*.

These sorts of processes are described in the relationship between the rabbit and the porcupine:

'The next day the sun was shining brightly.

"What a fine day to go down to the pond and catch some fish for supper!" said the Rabbit.

"Today we will clean house," the Porcupine said flatly. "We still have some left over beans for supper."

So they cleaned house and never got to go out in the sunshine at all. That evening the Rabbit had hiccups again from eating beans for supper, and a headache besides from being very annoyed and not daring to say so.

Slowly he was beginning to realize something else about his friend. It was not only difficult to disagree with the Porcupine. It was also impossible for the Porcupine *not* to disagree with *you*. No matter what you might say, he was sure to be contrary about it and do just the opposite.

If the Rabbit went to open the window, the Porcupine would exclaim, "No, no! I can't stand the draught. I'll be dead of pneumonia within the week."

If the Rabbit went to close the window, the Porcupine would gasp, "Air! I need fresh air!"

If the Rabbit started to make a fire in the fireplace, the Porcupine said they must not be wasteful with the firewood.

If the Rabbit thought it was too warm for a fire, the Porcupine accused him of being stingy with the firewood.'   (Annett 1971)

Family therapists will recognize such processes operating within all families, and will focus less on the content of such disagreements than on the repetitive and fixed roles adopted by participants. It is important to realize that individuals can become trapped in such roles through the pressure and the dynamics of the family system as a whole. Certain roles are complementary, and occur with regularity in families: a 'rescuer' will need a 'victim'; a 'victim' depends on a 'persecutor'; and so on.

Rejection of linear view of causality

In the classical model of science, causality is understood as being a linear process. Scientific examination establishes the 'cause' of an 'effect' by altering the variables one by one until the causal relationship is established. The model is that an identified stimulus produces an identified response.

Family therapists tend to adopt a view of causality as being *circular*, beginning from the premise that many significant aspects of an event or a series of events can only be understood by examining the activity – and the mutual influences – of the system as a whole. 'All parts of the organism form a circle. Therefore, every part is both beginning and end' (Hippocrates). An event or a piece of behaviour is not seen simply as the result of the influences which have directly preceded it. Causality is viewed as a sequence without beginning or end, and it becomes clear 'how close apparent opposites may be when we understand the basically circular nature of human experience' (Shands 1971).

Following from such views of circularity, the concept of *homeostasis* derived from systems theory as commonly applied to families has been described as follows:

'Systems theory postulates the existence of a network of inter-actions (the system) placed within an identifiable boundary. In close relation to the system is its environment (suprasystem), and its components and their inter-relationship (sub-systems). The dynamic element of the system is emphasized in that its constant movements and changes (e.g. reactions to the environment) are balanced and modified by the concept of homeo-stasis. The system has an inbuilt tendency to stability, including the capacity for stable adaptation and growth, and this stability is being constantly re-established by compensatory adjustments in the various parts and relationships of the system. . . .

To analyse the overall effect or efficiency of the system's operation consequently requires a view of the totality in action, examination of a part and its malfunction is not sufficient. The application to families of this theoretical concept is as ingenious as it is rewarding, even to therapists who do not wholly accept the orientation and some of the techniques of therapy which have developed from it. . . .

Of particular interest is the revelation that family members can actively or passively become afflicted with symptoms as a result of the efforts of the system to maintain or regain homeostasis. The inappropriate roles and role-reversals which frequently occur – and which are difficult to explain in terms of individual pathology, often assume a clear meaning when seen in the context of the interactions of the family as a whole.'

(Dale 1981)

Focus on the importance of communication

Family therapists see the unit for treatment as the whole family, although for various reasons this may not always be strictly adhered to in practice. Whole-family sessions not only provide the therapist with the opportunity to observe and influence family processes and rules, but also allow a view of patterns of *communication* within the family. Family therapists of all schools have an interest in the mechanics of communication, especially ways in which it gets blocked, distorted, or occurs covertly.

Non-verbal *behaviour* – including 'illness' and 'disturbance' – often has a communicative function in families where open channels are blocked. The family therapist seeks to make sense of the message behind the behaviour of a symptomatic member.

With physically and sexually abusing families, there are often very severe inhibitions and distortions in communication processes. In some inarticulate and highly frustrated families, violence may be the main channel, and an everyday occurrence between parents. Children quickly learn the rules of violent communication, and victims grow into aggressors. In some families violence to a child may be a desperate attempt at covert communication.

For example, we saw a family whose plans to emigrate to Australia had reached an advanced stage. The mother had gone along with her husband's enthusiastic planning. However, she had never allowed him to get in touch with her internal world which continued to involve an intense, hostile dependency on her own mother who lived nearby. As the day for departure approached her panic mounted as she could not bear to leave her mother or tell her husband. At this point one of the children was admitted to hospital with a severe inflicted injury. With the child in care, plans for emigration were abandoned.

The inhibition on communication in this family was typical of that in families where serious child abuse occurs. The danger to the child lay in the mother's inability to *tell* her husband of her fear of emigration, rather than in that fear itself. The husband played an *equal role* through a process of disqualifying and discounting anything that he did not wish to hear. The mother had a similar relationship with her own mother where equally dangerous covert communication patterns existed. There was an established *double-bind* communication trap: the mother would give verbal permission for the daughter to emigrate, but would non-verbally, and powerfully, contradict this – by illness, tone of voice, and role as 'martyr'.

In such situations family therapists would agree that a major part of the therapeutic task would be to intervene in the communication processes within the family. The ways in which this task would be approached would be quite different, as the next section will show.

Three models of family therapy

Historical family therapy

This school (sometimes referred to as 'analytic' family therapy) focuses predominantly on the reworking of past family events in the 'here and now'. In this sense there is a clear connection with the process of psychoanalysis, although the unit being treated is the whole family, not one individual. Family history is accorded important status as influencing the 'here and now' transactions, and *genograms* are often used in therapy to record and create an awareness of the continuing influence of the past on the current family problems. Genograms are pictorial representations of family histories and relationships compiled in the form of a family tree. Their use in assessments following child abuse is described in Chapter 5.

Hoffman (1981), in her excellent review of the development of the different family therapy models, comments on the similarities between historical family therapy and psychoanalysis regarding theories of change, goals of intervention, and techniques. Change is seen to occur through bringing out into the 'here and now' historically repressed or forbidden material, which may include a multi-generational 'family ledger' consisting of a system of obligations incurred and debts repaid over a long period of time. Byng-Hall (1973) described 'family myths' as powerful, unconscious processes which enable family members to remain unaware of significant, avoided themes. Bowen (1978) described a theory of the multi-generational transmission of emotional illness; this theory identifies the patterns originating in the past which exert a major influence over people in the present. The purpose of therapy is to enable individuals to unlock themselves from such historical entanglements, and to become more self-determining personalities.

It will be seen in later chapters that the historical model of family therapy has been an important influence on the work described in this book. Genograms are used both as a therapeutic tool and as a means of establishing the pattern of family *systems* over several generations. With many child-abusing families, genograms are useful in identifying the considerable 'unfinished business' left over from the parents' experience in their families of origin which often detrimentally affects their newly established parenting role.

A major purpose of family therapy of the historical school is to promote within each member (especially the member with the symptom) the development of an individual identity and independence, free from disabling historical emotional entanglements.

Therapists working within this broad framework would tend to adopt a less dominant and challenging style than family therapists with other orientations. Significant emotional change is likely to be seen as a fairly slow process. Family members are likely to be encouraged to work towards an ability to share and respond to powerful feelings instead of converting them into symptoms or other displacement activities.

Structural family therapy

Structural family therapy is described in the work of Salvador Minuchin whose influence is in fact even greater than is indicated by his considerable reputation both as a theorist and as a therapist. So many of Minuchin's concepts have been assimilated into common knowledge and practice that they are used without reference to, or even awareness of, their originator. Minuchin presented a normative model for a well-functioning family, in which the family system comprises three sub-systems: the spouse sub-system (parents alone); the parenting sub-system (parents and children); and the sibling sub-system (children alone). The family system is viewed as the total operation of the three sub-systems, all contained within a defined *boundary*, and existing within a specific cultural, social, and economic context.

The structural family therapist's first step is to 'join' with the family, to participate for a time in its transactions, and to observe its functioning. The attention of the therapist will be drawn to the structural processes operating within the family: to the strength or weaknesses of *boundaries* (both between the whole family and the extended family, and between the various sub-systems); to relationships of distance and proximity (the presence of alliances or scapegoats); and to the variety of *roles* which family members adopt. Inappropriate roles and role-reversals, which occur in families and are difficult to explain in terms of individual pathology, often assume a clear meaning when seen in the context of such structural relationships.

Stemming from this, structural therapists use an approach which tends to ignore the historical context of the family's 'problem', but which concentrates instead on the verbal and non-verbal *communication* taking place (or not taking place) in the 'here and now'. The approach involves the therapist as an energetic *intruder*, often exploiting charisma and personal power. The therapist works to actively restructure family organization and communication channels, less by interpretation than by modelling, the use of 'action-techniques', and direction.

The *active* component typifies structural family therapy, and is of particular value with families who are disabled in their use of language. This could mean either emotionally inarticulate families or over-articulate families who use words skilfully to avoid any real communication or the experience of real emotion.

Therapy on a non-verbal level can provide a powerful way of approaching significant issues through techniques such as *sculpting* or *enactment*. Sculpting involves family members portraying family relationships by means of literally arranging each member in a physical pose in a carefully considered proximity to each other person. The therapist will encourage that attention be paid to details such as gestures, facial expressions, and points of physical contact. Powerful representations of family life invariably emerge from sculpts, and it can be illuminating to allow each member the opportunity to demonstrate his or her own perceptions – significant differences often emerge!

Enactment is a technique whereby families may be requested to act out reported problems in the presence of the therapist. Whilst this is happening (and it can be surprising how quickly it does happen), the therapist can observe the part played by each family member, and can intervene to directly influence and alter these parts. Such interventions may involve an *intensification* of the scene being enacted, perhaps by a suggestion that the participants 'do more' of what they are doing, or 'do it harder'. Enactments quickly become very real emotionally, enabling the therapist to get into the heart of the difficulties and pain which the family is experiencing.

In work with child-abusing families where frequently issues of power and control are of crucial importance, the technique of enactment can be very valuable in allowing such conflicts to be experienced and explored in the safety of the therapeutic room.

Strategic family therapy

Strategic therapy, defined in the work of Erickson (Haley 1973), Watzlawick, Weakland, and Fisch (1974), and Palazzoli *et al.* (1980), disclaims interest in family structures or systems; in a way initially reminiscent of behaviour therapy, it adopts a primary focus on the problem. A major theoretical assumption is that the symptom is being maintained by the actions taken to remove it. In other words, the 'solution' comes to be an integral part of the problem.

Major techniques to promote change are 'positive connotation' and 'reframing'. These techniques allow the therapist to restate the problem so that it may be seen in a new way or in a different context. Reframing may involve a positive connotation – such as the anorectic girl's brave attempt and self-sacrifice to save her parents' marriage, or a critical parent's clear demonstration of commitment to the child. It is fundamental that reframing involves and addresses the role of each family member as to ways in which his or her behaviour contributes to and maintains the problem.

Following from reframing, another potent technique may be employed – that of *paradoxical injunctions*. At a simple level this involves an instruction to family members *not* to change or to 'do *more*' of the problem behaviour.

The Rabbit left his own house in despair at his domination by the contrary Porcupine. All of a sudden the wind blew an idea into his ear. The Rabbit returned home with a glimmer in his eye:

'That afternoon the Rabbit said, "I would like very much to have beans and brown bread for supper."

"That's too bad," the Porcupine snapped, "because we are going to have a salad of lettuce and carrots and cucumbers and radishes and cabbage."

In the evening it was a bit chilly. "Well, we can't have a fire tonight," the Rabbit said, "for we must not be wasteful with the firewood."

"Nonsense!" the Porcupine retorted. "What kind of home is it, if you can't be warm and cozy in it?" He proceeded at once to make a big fire.

And the Rabbit sat happily in his favourite chair next to the fireplace, nodding and dozing and toasting his toes.'

(Annett 1971)

In strategic family therapy, the power and potential for change lie in the family *resisting* the overt move by the therapist to take control of the symptoms. The only way successfully to thwart the therapist's instructions is to 'do *less*' of the problem behaviour. In response to this, further strategies may follow – the therapist may express disappointment that the family have failed to follow his 'expert' instruction; the therapist may 'fail' to recognize the positive changes which have occurred; or relapses may be predicted with the family being asked to anticipate the likely circumstances in which this might happen.

Central to strategic therapy is a view that the process of change involves a 'therapeutic contest' between the family and the therapist or therapeutic team. There is a belief in the fundamental power of families to render therapists impotent. To counter the power of the family, the team is likely to make use of live consultation by colleagues through a one-way screen.

At the same time, the therapists will aim to maintain a stance of *neutrality* in their dealings with each family member, so that there can be no perception by the family that the therapist has been drawn into an alliance or supporting position with any particular member. The technique of *circular questioning* is central to maintaining therapeutic neutrality. In circular questioning, family members are asked to comment on the behaviour, attitudes, and relationships of *other* members, not themselves. This change in approach alone can be very potent, especially for families which trade in well-rehearsed, self-reported 'feelings', and attract a succession of therapists who deal in them, without any change ever occurring.

Circular questioning is aimed at establishing *differences*, and definitions of relationships, often through requesting ratings or comparisons between family members over important issues. The following types of questions are examples: 'Who is the most worried about the problem?'; 'Who is the second most worried?'; 'What is the biggest problem in the family?'; 'How worried is each member – on a scale of 0 to 10?'; 'What does X do when Y is worried/sick/angry?' This style of interviewing not only approaches very significant areas, but also has the therapeutically desirable effect of beginning to unbalance the homeostasis of the family system. Strategic therapists recognize that family systems often become locked into unsatisfying sets of relationships, which nevertheless provide the most comfortable roles for the family members to exist within. Powerful processes exist within families to sustain distorted transactions, no matter how unsatisfying to members they may be.

Strategic therapy has attracted criticism on account of the seemingly distant, less compassionate, or even 'cold' role adopted by the therapists. In our experience, such criticism tends to come from workers whose own therapeutic stance is more concerned with being 'nice' to people than with helping them to change.

From these brief portrayals of some aspects of the different schools of family therapy, their influence on the work of the team described in this book will become apparent in the following chapters. However, this account of therapeutic influences cannot close without reference to the experientially based therapy of *Gestalt*.

Gestalt

The word *Gestalt* refers to the concept of a 'whole', or a 'completion', or an 'integrated pattern', where the whole is more than the sum of the parts. The creator of *Gestalt* therapy, Fritz Perls, was originally trained in psychoanalysis, but rejected the lengthy process of historically based treatment. In contrast, *Gestalt* therapy is an emotionally intense, but much shorter-term, process. Perls subscribed strongly to the humanistic belief in the inborn healthiness of every individual, and followed the influence of existential philosophy which stressed each individual's responsibility for his or her own situation.

Gestalt therapy is fundamentally an experiential process in which the emphasis is on physical and emotional *awareness*, rather than on any thinking or cognitive activity. Therapy discourages clients from intellectualizing or interpreting their lives in an abstract or detached way. Instead the therapist encourages the client to bring personal issues into a 'here and now' awareness, and to explore and perhaps intensify the associated emotions, or to explore the blocks which arise to keep such emotions outside full awareness.

The persistent focus on what the client is experiencing *now* (and what he is avoiding experiencing) promotes the important process by which each individual takes responsibility for and *owns* what he or she feels, and takes decisions in respect of available options. By owning feelings, experiences, and actions, individuals begin to experience increased 'response-ability', and begin to make the transition from being passive recipients of life events to being active participants in life.

Within *Gestalt* therapy there is an unlimited array of experiential therapeutic techniques – unlimited, as the ingenuity of the therapist is based to a large extent on his own intuitive and emotional response to the client within a framework of basic techniques. It is an important principle that the therapist must have experienced the techniques used from the position of client. *Gestalt* techniques are not simply to be learned and applied – their effectiveness stems from the shared experience of therapist and client.

Some basic Gestalt techniques

Therapy is based on the premise that the therapist provides a safe context for the *client* to do the work, which will involve taking emotional risks. The therapist will make constant use of his own emotional experience of the client as he attends to verbal and non-verbal signals.

Non-verbal attentiveness

It is not unusual in the area of child abuse for the therapist to encounter parents with disastrous emotional histories and for these to spill out readily in initial encounters. Often the client will have told the same story to a number of different people, without any change having occurred. It can be useful for the therapist to interrupt such outpourings in such a way as to encourage an awareness of a less obvious aspect of the experience. This could mean drawing the client's attention to a tapping foot, or a clenched fist, or a recurrent facial gesture. What is the non-verbal gesture communicating? It may be useful to stop the verbal account and ask the client to exaggerate the non-verbal gesture, and then to focus on immediate emotional responses. Often, buried emotional experiences relating back to unacknowledged 'unfinished business' will come into the client's consciousness and provide a very different – and more authentic – emotional tone to the matters which he or she had been relating.

Another way of intensifying the emotional effect or of promoting a more authentic emotional effect is to suggest to the client that he describes an important historical event *as if it were happening now*. One father's earliest memory was of lying in his pram, totally bored, and wishing that someone would attend to him. Nobody came. In a *Gestalt* session he re-experienced this event as if it were happening in the present. With some encouragement he experimented with making a lot of noise, and demanding that he be attended to. He began to experience getting in touch with a powerfully suppressed anger.

This technique is especially productive with personalities who have long ago learned to over-control and suppress important emotions, and who instead have developed a range of displacement activities.

Linguistic techniques

Some very simple principles can make enormous changes in therapeutic progress. These are to do with promoting an increased awareness in clients of their ability to take decisions and make choices. The therapist can insist on the client making 'I' statements, discouraging the use of terms such as 'one feels', 'everybody wants', 'we always'. Instead the therapist will suggest that such statements *whenever* they occur be restated as 'I feel', 'I want', and 'I always'.

A similar process occurs when the therapist suggests that the words 'will not' be substituted whenever clients say they 'cannot'; that they say they 'want' every time they say they 'need'; and that they say 'and' in situations where they habitually use 'but'. For example, 'I would like to leave him and stop being beaten but I would be lonely'. This phrasing consolidates inaction. However, 'I would like to leave him and stop being beaten *and* I will be lonely' implies choice with potential in the untried possibility.

Fantasy dialogues (or, 'It's bloody silly to talk to a chair')

For many people, *Gestalt* therapy has tended to be notorious for the technique of *talking to the cushion* (it doesn't have to be a chair). The technique is based on the *Gestalt* conception of splits within the personality which can move towards integration through an exploration of their differences. Everybody experiences such splits on a simple day-to-day basis: at this moment, whilst writing, 'part' of me wants to stop and watch an interesting programme on television; another 'part' of me wants to get this chapter finished before I go on holiday in two days' time and feels that it *should* carry on writing. I could decide to pause and set up a dialogue between these two parts, and explore the complex issues of awareness and motivation which will lie behind the surface of each. I suspect that quickly I would get in touch with important historical issues of unfinished business to do with ambivalence about ambition.

The use of this technique is often associated with a focus on the mechanisms of projection utilized by the client. The dynamic is that characteristics which a person does not like in him or herself are denied and attributed to others. Therapy will utilize experiments geared to help the client experience the projected element of self – re-owning the projection and integrating that emotion into the personality. For example people who experience themselves as always being criticized by others may be encouraged to act out being very critical. A dialogue may be established between the two parts. Change occurs following the genuine experience of the critical faculty within the personality which had been denied.

The same technique can be used for difficulties in interpersonal relationships, and interpersonal as well as intrapsychic conflict can be tackled by the use of two chairs or cushions to embody the polarized positions. Dialogues develop, encouraged by the therapist, and regular switching from cushion to cushion occurs as the emotional intensity heightens. Such exchanges are likely to culminate in cathartic experiences, and quite battered cushions.

Using cushions in this way to deal with unfinished business from previous family relationships can be of considerable benefit for individuals within child-abusing families. For example, in situations where the mechanism appears to be 'I'm doing to her what was done to me', the force of the anger can often be redirected back on to the family of origin – via the cushions – and away from the child who had become the unfortunate focus. One mother in such a situation, in the context of an agreed number of *Gestalt* sessions, ultimately beat a symbolic paper representation of her father to death with a shoe. When asked what she was going to do with the body, she ripped the paper carefully into minute shreds, placed it in a wastepaper basket, and set fire to it. She then sat transfixed for several minutes watching him burn, before finally saying, 'It's over'.

The work described in this book was carried out by a team originally orientated in family therapy, but increasingly influenced by *Gestalt* theory and therapeutic techniques. *Gestalt* therapy offers a 'tool kit' of experiential techniques which provide powerful 'here and now' opportunities for the re-solving of historical and current issues of 'unfinished business' within and between individuals. It provides an often intense emotional component to therapy which can be especially appropriate to over-controlling families, and which is often missing from many family therapy techniques. Throughout this book, it will be stressed that there are forces which can lure professionals who have the best of intentions into taking inappropriate stances with child-abusing families, and thus adding to the existing dynamics of dangerousness.

This chapter has described the historical context within which the assessment and therapeutic work of the Rochdale NSPCC team developed. Chapter 2 stresses the importance of considering wider systems and establishing a basic level of protection for the child, before assessment of the family begins.

CHAPTER 2

Dangerousness: Families and professionals

Little William without a doubt
Pulled his baby's eyeballs out.
Jumped on them to make them pop,
Daddy said, "Now William, stop."

Willie, with a thirst for gore,
Nailed his sister to the door.
Mother said, with humour quaint:
"Willie dear, don't scratch the paint."

(Traditional rhymes)

There is a remarkable lack of literature and research on the assessment and future management of families in which a child has been criminally killed or seriously injured. Although many important lessons have been learned from the succession of public inquiries into fatal child abuse, it is unfortunate that little attention has been paid to the pathological dynamics within the families. The inquiries provide chronological accounts of the crescendo of events, but are framed within a search to understand the relationship between the family and the professional agencies, consequently missing the opportunity to extend our understanding of the specific transactions within these families which resulted in fatal child abuse.

Much of the literature which has examined significant factors found in seriously child-abusing families has included attempts to construct predictive devices or 'checklists' to identify high-risk families. Such indicators may be extremely comprehensive, covering a wide range of social, medical, intrapsychic, and interpersonal features. Unfortunately, whilst such characteristics are invariably identified retrospectively in cases of child abuse, and as such can indicate a general and very large high-risk group, they are far too imprecise to assist in making specific child-protection assessments.

Dangerous individuals

Research literature on dangerousness has mainly been concerned with studies of adult-to-adult violence based on the characteristics of violent offenders in prison or secure psychiatric hospitals. This research demonstrates that indicators of dangerousness are poor and unrefined. The best single indicator of future violence is previous violence, but even this is more likely to be wrong than right (Walker 1978). No standard definition of dangerousness exists. Hamilton (1982) preferred the simple 'potential to cause serious physical harm to others', although he accepted that there is a case for psychological harm to be included as well. Monahan and Cummings (1975) outlined the extent of judicial preventive detention in the United States based on *psychiatric predictions* of dangerousness, stating that this affected some 50,000 people each year.

The inadequacy of powers of prediction means a major moral dilemma for social policy in this area: whether to release offenders who may then commit violent acts again, or whether to keep them in detention, even though they might not reoffend if released. Greenland (1980b) quoted the medical director of a maximum-security hospital who said that only about 10 per cent of his patients would kill again on discharge – he would be delighted to release the remaining 90 per cent if someone could tell him, reliably, who they are. The continued unnecessary detention of patients in such circumstances reflects the problem of the *overprediction* of violence – the false positives.

Monahan and Cummings (1975) referred to studies which showed an alarming rate of overprediction of violence. Stating a range of error of between 54 per cent and 99 per cent in some studies, they argued for caution in, if not restriction of, the use of such predictors for prodromal identification and treatment. Walker (1978) argued that if we accept that the tendency to error is strongly in the direction of false positives, and that decisions are taken with good intentions on the best use of available information, then mistakes are regrettable – but not morally wrong.

Although in the literature most of the dilemmas described relate to the sentencing, detention, and release of violent offenders against adults, most of the concerns are the same as those found within the field of the prediction and prevention of child abuse. Just as the issue of compulsory psychiatric treatment consistently arouses passionate ethical debates, the question of prodromal identification and preventive protective action – for example the removal of babies from their parents at birth – is an area of acutely delicate moral balance.

Incidence and indicators

In 1970 in Great Britain there were about 130 murders known to the police. One-third of the victims were children under the age of sixteen, of whom three-quarters were killed by a parent or parents. In the same year, 82 per cent of all murders were committed by men. However, for parents who had killed their own children, the position was reversed: only 15 per cent of male murderers had killed their own child, whereas 69 per cent of women murderers had done so (Scott 1973).

It is useful to contrast the corresponding figures over the subsequent decade. Home Office statistics are now presented collectively as 'homicide', which covers the offences of murder, manslaughter, and infanticide. In 1971, offences currently recorded as homicide in England and Wales numbered 407. Of these homicides of children aged under sixteen by their parents numbered 101 or 25 per cent. In 1981, the number of homicides was 517, of which fifty-three were of children under the age of sixteen killed by their parents – 10 per cent. In 1983, the number of homicides was 506, of which fifty-four or 11 per cent were of children under the age of sixteen killed by their parents (Home Office Criminal Statistics). (The term 'parent' in these statistics includes natural parent, stepparent, foster parent, adoptive parent, and cohabitant of any of these.)

In Britain there has been some controversy about the figures relating to fatal child abuse, and a good deal of debate about the accuracy of statistics. It is important to note that this is not peculiar to Britain. At the Fifth International Congress on Child Abuse and Neglect (Montreal, September, 1984) it was stated that the number of confirmed child abuse deaths per year in the state of California was some 150 in a population of 25 million. The Californian child-protective agencies considered that this was a gross underestimate, and that the real figure was at least three times greater. Compare this with the disputed British figures of between 50 and 100 child abuse deaths per year in a population of 55 million (Dale 1985).

Many workers in Britain also feel that the real incidence of fatal child abuse is understated, particularly since many highly suspicious deaths of children in families where abuse is previously known to have occurred are not recorded as homicides because there may have been insufficient evidence for a criminal conviction. Many child abuse practitioners have also had the experience of working with parents who some years later acknowledge a degree of responsibility for the death of a child which at the time was recorded as accidental or due to natural causes. Even so, there is cause for a good deal of satisfaction that the official figures record a 50 per cent reduction in cases of fatal child abuse over the last decade. The most likely cause of this significant decrease is the vastly improved efficiency and effectiveness of inter-agency child abuse management systems, together with increased awareness and skill on the part of all relevant professions to identify cases at an early stage and to take effective protective action to prevent the classic spiral of repeated minor injuries becoming serious and ultimately fatal.

It comes as no surprise to child-protection workers of all disciplines that such demonstrable achievements are never featured by the popular media, which continue to base their sensation-seeking sales campaigns on the public pillorying of professionals involved in the latest fatal child abuse scandal.

Scott (1973) studied twenty-nine men who were charged with killing a child under the age of five and who presented significant family, social, and psychiatric factors. Two-thirds of the men were not married to their partner, and half of them were not the biological father of the victim. There was a high prevalence of abnormal behaviour or mental illness in their own families, and twenty of the men had a significant personality disorder. Nearly all experienced recognizable difficulty in controlling themselves and in coping with stress, and 27 per cent had a previous history of violent crime. Three-quarters had given *unmistakable warning* of their subsequent action but were at the time and subsequently *protected by the partner*. In one-half of the cases there was serious delay in seeking help for the child. All blamed the victim for the immediate precipitation of the attack, citing disobedience, refusal to smile or to learn, being wet or dirty – thus reflecting the *unrealistic expectations of the parents*.

Greenland (1980b) agreed with Scott's identification of the presence of unmistakable warnings given by the perpetrator before the violent act. He postulated from his own research that the impulse to kill is almost invariably accompanied by an equal but opposite urge to be restrained from killing. He concluded that 'the lengths to which some patients will go to avoid killing others is extraordinary'. The phenomenon of 'help-seeking' and 'warning behaviour' on the part of potential perpetrators is fundamental but is often tragically ignored by professionals and family members alike.

Many researchers have addressed themselves to the *motives* involved in fatal child abuse, in an attempt to establish a form of classification which distinguishes between different types of cases. Resnick (1969) produced a five-point classification: (1) altruistic killing to relieve the victim's realistic or delusional suffering, whether or not followed by suicide; (2) acute psychosis; (3) elimination of an unwanted child, e.g. when paternity is in doubt, or it would mean financial burden; (4) accidental or unconscious motivation in which the homicidal intent is lacking; (5) spouse revenge – the Medea situation (following desertion by her husband, Medea killed their two children, saying, 'Thy sons are dead and gone, that will stab thy heart').

Scott felt that classifications based on motive were weak, because motivation is highly subjective and may be constructed retrospectively in a defensive way. He concluded that:

'Direct observation of murderers suggests that the majority commit the offence when their higher controls of discretion, reason, sympathy, and self-criticism are more or less in abeyance, and when they are acting at so primitive a level that such

motives as revenge and altruism may be quite inappropriate.'
(Scott 1973: 121)

Scott also addressed the discussion surrounding the influence of aggression in the perpetrators of fatal child abuse whom he studied. His view was that the two most common sources of aggression are learning and frustration. With the habitually aggressive, the individual is likely to have learned that the aggression is rewarding in that other people can be influenced to behave in a way which achieves desired ends. In the process the individual is likely to have learned how far to go with it, and how to use aggression to best advantage, and consequently to have acquired considerable *control*. Scott commented that: 'This may explain why the so-called "aggressive psychopaths", on follow up, are not found to have been particularly aggressive . . . the aggressive psychopath, while he often frightens people and makes a great nuisance of himself, rarely kills' (Scott 1973: 121).

This observation fits with other evidence which recognizes that it is the quiet, over-inhibited individual who is the most dangerously aggressive. The unexpected violence in the otherwise passive personality is certainly a feature of many fatal cases of child abuse.

Research into family violence has indicated clearly many of the important factors involved in the syndrome of child abuse. A range of checklists has been produced in an attempt to identify accurately high-risk families. What is lacking is a more systematic way of indicating, within the very large high-risk groups which emerge, the families which do indeed pose an immediate and serious threat to the life and safety of a child. This book will suggest that important, significant information in this respect can be gained from the viewpoint of how the entire family operates as a system.

Dangerous families

Although as parents we habitually warn our children of the dangers which may be posed by strangers with evil intentions, it is an unpleasant reality that the vast proportion of children who are seriously physically assaulted or sexually abused are victims within their family environment. Of the seventy-eight children currently recorded as victims of homicide in England and Wales in 1983, sixty-nine (88 per cent) were killed by a parent or other family member, or a friend, acquaintance, or other associate. Only three of the children were killed by strangers. The six remaining killings are unsolved.

Violence to children therefore needs to be considered primarily within the context of the family. In our experience – and a thorough reading of all the public inquiry reports into cases of fatal child abuse supports this view – incidents of serious child abuse invariably involve a triangular relationship between the perpetrator, the victim, and the partner who adopts the role of 'failure to protect' the child. It is this 'failure to protect' role which is often such a perplexing aspect of an inquiry, and so misleading for many professionals attempting to work with such families. Agencies are often unwittingly led into a collusive singular focus on the behaviour of the aggressor, and fail to appreciate the deep pathology within the partner who chooses not to act on warning signs, or who actively supports an escalating process of child cruelty until the point of no return is reached, and the fatal outcome becomes inevitable. Such dynamics operating within this dangerous family triangle are described in Chapter 5, and are illustrated throughout the book in case examples.

In 1985, the year in which this book was written, Britain again witnessed a succession of quite horrendous, fatal child abuse cases in consequence of which the public were again jolted into awareness of the extent to which parents can be systematically and sadistically cruel to their children. The cases of *Tyra Henry* (who died from severe brain injuries, and whose body also showed fifty-seven human bite marks inflicted by her father) and *Jasmine Beckford* (a child who had previously suffered serious abuse and was returned home from foster care to be persistently neglected and then fatally injured) aroused particular public disquiet, as both were killed whilst living with their parents and still subject to care orders.

The name of *Heidi Koseda* was added to the roll of horror not only because of the almost unbelievable barbarity of her treatment by her parents (Heidi was locked in a dismal dark room and literally starved to death; she tried to keep alive by eating wallpaper. Her body lay in the room for two months whilst her parents continued their normal life) but also because of the failure of a child-protective agency – in this case the NSPCC – to take appropriate action following reports of acute concern from a neighbour. The director of the NSPCC immediately and unreservedly acknowledged the responsibility of the society for its tragic failing in this case.

Professional dangerousness

Whilst some features of dangerousness within families and individuals have been presented, it is important to recognize that this is not the whole story. Individuals and families exist within a network of professionals and agencies which provide their own contribution to the dynamics of risk. Public inquiries have repeatedly shown that inadequate child abuse management procedures, or failure to comply with satisfactory ones, are often major features of the professionals' role in cases where fatal abuse has occurred. Additional to the procedural issues is the equally important but largely unexpressed question of how the personal emotional resources of the individual professional workers affect their performance. The level of such resources is crucial – inasmuch as a professional judgement based on perception is critically affected by degrees of alertness, energy, and creativity, or their opposites, lethargy, depression, and burn-out.

The issue of professional stress is fundamental, and as crucial to effective child protection as the absence of delirium tremens to a successful brain surgeon. Professionals operating from a position of chronic stress are highly susceptible to errors of omission – not taking all possible action to ensure the safety of a child at a crucial moment.

Professionals also experience significant personal stress from the highly charged emotional issues thrown up by child-abusing families. It is of great significance that the experience of being a child abuse victim is not restricted to 'clients', but affects a significant number of professionals who work with such families. In a confidential survey of a large number of professionals taking part in our training courses on physical and sexual abuse, 20 per cent of all participants reported having been sexually abused during childhood, and 15 per cent reported a personal history of being physically abused in childhood. It seems clear that part of the motivation for many professionals to 'help' others involves a private confrontation with significant personal issues.

It is not easy for professionals to declare their own personal agendas and how these relate to their chosen sphere of work. They fear a disqualificatory and undermining response from managers and colleagues – many of whom are themselves only pretending to be emotionally strong. In the same survey, 65 per cent of the professionals stated that they felt that they would benefit from a therapeutic relationship within which to review their own personal issues to do with physical and sexual abuse. A crucial maxim for all professionals is 'Get help for yourselves'. Most of us are struggling or have struggled with the same issues.

Dangerous professionals

It is possible to caricature types of behaviour of dangerous professionals. For example, the 'dangerous social worker' may be best illustrated by the picture of a worker, operating alone and in isolation, attempting to make contact with an unenthusiastic or hostile family in respect of some expressed concerns that the children may be in some way 'at risk'. Such approaches may be made by focusing on more mutually acceptable problem areas such as housing or material benefits, as neither the worker nor the family feels comfortable with an open statement of the real concern.

The next phase occurs when, having provided a nursery place, the social worker is informed that the child regularly appears in the nursery with increasingly suspicious minor bruising, perhaps to the cheeks, upper arms, or chest. The referral is likely to have been delayed by a dangerous officer in charge. The dangerous social worker will then either reluctantly (and very anxiously) visit the parents to enquire about the bruising, but will be eager to accept rather implausible explanations. At the extreme, the dangerous social worker will refuse to investigate (supported by a dangerous manager), rationalizing that the referral is too late, and also that it would 'damage my relationship with the family'. This is one of the catch-phrases of the dangerous social worker in action – although it is also regularly observed in the dangerous health visitor. When noted it should cause immediate alarm and prompt active review of the management of the case. A 'relationship' which can be 'damaged' in such a way is in fact only a relationship of enmeshment and collusion: the antithesis of any therapeutic or supervisory contact. A professional relationship which cannot include the discussion of real concerns inevitably reveals itself on examination as not a relationship at all, but an avoidance of conflict and difference.

In such situations the dangerous social worker – often as the result of inadequate training – is operating without any consistent theoretical base from which to understand the dynamics of child abuse, and usually with no sound conception of therapeutic possibilities. The dangerous social worker will often focus exclusively on the solution of material problems, and adopt what Dingwall, Eekelaar, and Murray (1983) described as the 'rule of optimism' – hoping that the resulting reduction in stress will significantly alter family dynamics. In this context, continuing minor injuries are tolerated and over-optimistically interpreted, rather than being viewed as significant warning signs.

The 'dangerous health visitor', also in caricature, is likely to fall unknowingly into an enmeshed and highly collusive relationship with client families. This often stems from a heavy *personal* investment in an inadequately formulated 're-parenting' therapeutic model which has become fixated at the level of acceptance and nurturing. The dangerous health visitor – for the covert satisfaction of her own needs to give and be accepted – adopts an over-ambitious, over-optimistic, and therefore exhausting parental role towards the family and all aspects of its life. The more the dangerous health visitor 'helps' and 'accepts', the more demanding and disturbed the family's relationships become. The scene becomes one in which the parents either adopt a position of passive, total dependency (which conceals a denied resentment) or else constantly escalate their demands, using their children as veiled hostages, their safety implicitly dependent on the health visitor's continued co-operating. In such situations an intolerable anxiety is created as exhaustion mounts, and the health visitor begins to realize that the more she parents the family, the more demanding they become. As her commitment falters, the parents are likely to switch from their position of passive aggression into one of quite ferocious criticism and persecution which leaves the dangerous health visitor with intense feelings of rejection – if not a serious personal emotional crisis.

Although presented in caricature through the perspectives of dangerous social workers and dangerous health visitors, the phenomenon of the blurring of boundaries between personal needs and professional roles is something which affects practitioners of all disciplines. The worker becomes over-involved and over-identified with the family, and through constant exposure (such as daily visiting) to the minutiae of family matters is quite unable to see the direction of family processes or the significance of certain events. Such contact may be described as being a 'friend' to the family, and usually stems from the over-application of an unplanned nurturing therapeutic model which barely conceals the extent of the professional's own need to be cared for. Essentially, the unmet needs of such practitioners are so great that they have become 'helpaholics'.

Brandon (1976) addressed such processes of therapeutic *hindering*, commenting that: 'Helping and caring for others can be a very effective way of concealing desperate personal needs. It can conceal a need to control and even punish others. We may seek to be adequate in the face of the inadequacy of others' (Brandon 1976: 33).

Stevens (1971) also addressed the question of whose needs are really being met during the therapeutic process:

' "Helping" – one of the commonest (and also widely accepted) ways of not respecting a person's experience is to rush in with help when a person is feeling "bad" or uncomfortable. Being "helpful" with reassurance, jokes, comfort, etc., prevents the person from fully experiencing his grief, anger, aloneness, etc. Only through experiencing it fully can he accept it, assimilate it into his total life experience, and grow into a more complete and integrated human being. Almost always the "helper" actually helps *himself* by helping others. By rushing in with a band-aid, he stops the expression of feelings which are painful for *him* to feel. He also convinces himself and others that he is capable of helping others and doesn't need help himself. Almost every "helper" has strong feelings of helplessness which diminish temporarily when he helps someone else. This is true of a great many people in the "helping" professions: teachers, psychologists, and especially social workers. If you have this symptom, you will have to explore it in yourself and accept your own feelings of helplessness before you can really help others.'

(Stevens 1971: 128)

Another form of professional dangerousness occurs with practitioners who hold a rigid, stereotypical view of people and the problems they experience, and who also, underlying this, lack the ability to make genuine emotional contact with other human beings. This experience may often be the point of entry of the dangerous doctor, who is liable to be especially perilous when he has assimilated from his personality and training the view that his judgement is infallible. He is particularly liable to confuse medical knowledge with personal wisdom.

A notable example is a family doctor to whom a ten-week-old baby had been referred by the health visitor on no less than seven separate occasions because of unexplained facial bruising. Each time the doctor told the health visitor that although he agreed that the parents' explanations did not seem to account for the recurring bruising adequately, it could not be child abuse as the parents were 'nice people'. It was necessary to advise the health visitor on the next occasion to bypass the family doctor and take the baby directly to an experienced paediatrician. This action, together with the social work investigation which followed, revealed an extremely fraught family where the father had been thumping the crying baby during the night. The mother had been aware of this but took no protective action. Once the reality of the problem was revealed – to great parental relief – it was possible to provide both protection for the child and therapeutic help for the family; there were no further incidents for concern.

Such caricatures and examples of dangerous social workers, dangerous health visitors, and dangerous doctors can easily be continued with numerous anecdotes, and applied equally to other professions. Readers will be able to create their own visions of dangerous teachers, psychologists, nurses, police, etc. It is of vital importance that all agencies provide sufficient training and channels of emotional support for professionals who are involved in the management and treatment of child-abusing families, and also that professionals become comfortable in recognizing and expressing their needs in these areas. Ultimately, only professionals who are able to recognize and deal with their own stress responses will be able to provide and sustain effective protective and therapeutic intervention for families under severe stress.

Inter-agency dangerousness

> Susie had a baby
> She called him Tiny Tim
> She put him in the bathtub
> To see if he could swim
> He drank up all the water
> He ate up all the soap
> He tried to eat the bathtub
> But it wouldn't go down his throat.
> Susie called the doctor
> Susie called the nurse
> Susie called the lady with the alligator purse.
> Mumps said the doctor
> Measles said the nurse
> Chickenpox said the lady with the alligator purse.
> Out went the doctor
> Out went the nurse
> Out went the lady with the alligator purse.
>
> (Traditional rhyme)

Perhaps the most dangerous aspect of inter-agency functioning lies in the ways in which agencies relate to one another. Relationships between agencies reflect the same patterns of behaviour as normal and abnormal families: there are healthy conflicts and rivalries; clear and blurred boundaries; alliances and scapegoats; overt and covert communication patterns; and the operation of supportive, provocative, and even destructive patterns of behaviour. From such observations it is clear that inter-agency conflicts can sometimes seriously interfere with the successful identification, treatment, and management of child-abusing families. Covert issues between agencies, which may become apparent in certain forums such as case-conferences, may seriously contaminate the formal problem-solving activity of the whole inter-agency system. On occasions, the inter-agency system may require more thera-peutic time than the family, or may require a decisive intervention before productive therapeutic work with a family can begin. An example showing the importance of such issues is presented in Chapter 6.

Case-conferences

The concept of dangerousness is just as applicable to the behaviour of individuals within agencies as to relationships between agencies. Classical organizational theory provides many insights into what may be considered dangerous behaviour. The research project on the Hawthorne factory in the United States, for instance, revealed a distinction between 'formal' and 'informal' organization (Roethlisberger and Dickson 1949). The former is the blueprint of prescriptive rules by which an organization works, whilst the latter is what actually happens – how individuals put the rules into operation and how they can subvert or ignore them.

Gouldner (1954) illustrated how once an organization, or individuals within organizations, are in the grip of 'informal' processes, the tightening of prescriptive rules does not resolve the problem – indeed it may exacerbate the difficulty. One extremely important consequence of this in the arena of child abuse management is that increasingly tight application of formal prescriptive rules (e.g. child abuse procedures) in an attempt to eradicate bad practice and informal operations is likely to be ineffective and even counter-productive. Procedures alone cannot eliminate bad practice, although they are crucial when linked to appropriate multi-disciplinary training.

Case-conferences constitute a formal forum at which professional workers share information about a family; they are additional to the informal contacts which take place continually. In Rochdale, members of the NSPCC Child Protection Team chair and minute all the child abuse case-conferences in the borough. It is essential that an accurate, written record of the case-conference discussion and recommendations should be produced and circulated promptly to all participants and others who convey apologies for absence.

Child abuse case-conferences will be convened in a variety of circumstances. An urgent meeting may be held following a child's admission to hospital; it will be necessary to formulate a plan for the child's (and siblings') immediate safety whilst further investigations – perhaps by the police – take place. Such conferences will address the issue of basic child protection: will this child (and siblings) be at further risk if allowed to return home immediately? If so, are there sufficient grounds upon which to apply for a place of safety order? Is the injury serious enough to require a police investigation?

Having dealt satisfactorily with issues of initial management, and afforded the children in the family adequate protection, the conference may reconvene at a later stage to consider the most effective way of providing help to the whole family in respect of the problems identified from the investigation. It may be, as in the majority of cases described in this book, that the children have been made subject to care orders and an assessment has been requested from the NSPCC team to recommend whether the children can return home. When such assessments are completed, the work will be presented in some detail to a further conference, as it is essential that all agencies should be able to follow through the work the family has undertaken and recognize the changes they have made. It is crucial that the inter-agency system can move with the family's progress, and not remain fixated in the opinions it held at the time of the initial conference.

Child abuse case-conferences should routinely consider the situation of *each* child within the family, including as much observation from different professionals as possible. The social workers' observations of the children within the home should always be matched with information from their schools and from the health visitor who should have detailed observations of the physical (including growth rates and weights) and emotional development of pre-school children. Not only are such observations crucial when considering the question of specific evidence for care proceedings, but when collated over time they provide clear indications of *trends* in child behaviour and development which at a later stage may constitute significant legal evidence.

Case-conferences also regularly reveal significant *gaps* in information – for example the criminal record of a 'friend' or 'lodger' temporarily staying with a family. In families where child abuse has occurred such 'friends' are often found to have significant criminal records of violence against children, and as such to be Schedule 1 offenders. A Schedule 1 offence in itself is one of the primary grounds for care proceedings (see Chapter 3). 'Roving cohabitees' with records of violence prey on the susceptibilities of immature, lonely single mothers who may be unaware of such criminal backgrounds and the consequent risk to their own children.

Case-conferences also provide a forum for agencies to review the effects of multi-agency involvement with a particular family.

Often multi-agency involvement is indicated, and with appropriate liaison, roles and tasks can be kept distinct and observable progress made. However, on many occasions multi-agency involvement can become totally confused and competitive, with considerable hostility developing between the various professionals. Effective chairmanship of case-conferences can often significantly promote positive change in such circumstances, through the use of very similar techniques to those described throughout this book in relation to work with disturbed families!

In addition to attempting to understand and assess risk in families, case-conferences enable each professional to clarify his or her own precise role, and to look at how this fits in with the roles of others. Inevitably, as a reflection of the level of anxiety which surrounds much child abuse work, professionals will also feel a need to share responsibilities and be concerned with issues of self- and agency protection. At the end of any conference, the chairman will clarify the outcome of the discussion in terms of the recommendations reached, noting any dissensions. Case-conference recommendations are exactly that, and the professional discretion and legal responsibilities of any agency are not restricted in any way. Professionals and agencies should not be bound into a particular course of action with their options limited or prescribed by a case-conference. Safe, effective, and creative practice is not engendered by tight, formal regulation, but through responsible and responsive inter-agency relationships between professionals who have had the opportunity to share with each other and clarify their understanding and anxieties about a family.

Our experience of chairing over 2,000 child abuse case-conferences over a period of five years highlighted some of the difficulties encountered in the operation of such a formal system. Of crucial importance is the recognition that the processes operating in the conference may be more powerful than the issues being discussed. In caricature, the activity 'on top' of the table – the discussion about the family – may be seriously affected by the simultaneous activity 'below the table'. The covert activity 'below the table' may include a wide range of power struggles, status and experience differences, and undeclared personal agendas.

Given the multiple functions of a case-conference – to plan immediate protection of a child; to formulate longer-term assessment and treatment plans; to provide a forum for professional disagreements to be resolved and anxieties shared – it is unlikely that there will be any more efficient or productive formal meeting than the confidential, multi-disciplinary case-conference, not attended by the family. This is not to suggest in any way that relevant information and concerns about the family should not be conveyed to them; a conference will usually agree that a specific professional should undertake this task soon after the meeting.

It may be that there are strong arguments for having case-conferences with the family present. Our view is that this would enable *certain* of the case-conference tasks to be carried out but that other essential issues would be left for separate, informal professional contacts, and so a two-tier system of communication would develop. In addition, such meetings would become professionally diluted, as many professional groups have consistently indicated that they would not attend.

This argument for case-conferences excluding parental participation is *not* to suggest that parents should be excluded from other types of formal meetings. Indeed the model of network meetings described below evolved partly as a way of *increasing* parental influence and involvement within the professional system.

Network meetings

'Once upon a time there was a little chicken called Chicken Licken. One day an acorn fell from a tree and hit Chicken Licken on the head.

Chicken Licken thought that the sky was falling down. . . . So he ran off to tell the king.

On the way he met Henny Penny and told her that the sky was falling in and that they must go and tell the king. So they rushed off together. . . .

On the way they met . . . Cocky Locky . . . and . . . Ducky Lucky . . . and . . . Drakey Lakey . . . and . . . Goosey Loosey . . . and . . . Turkey Lurkey . . . and they all hurried on to tell the king that the sky was falling down.

Then they met Foxy Loxy. "Oh! Foxy Loxy!" said Chicken Licken. "The sky is falling down and we are on our way to tell the king."

"I know where to find the king," said Foxy Loxy. "You had better all follow me."

Foxy Loxy led them straight into his den, where his wife and their little foxes were waiting for their dinners. . . .

So Chicken Licken never found the king to tell him that he thought the sky was falling down.'

(Ladybird Books 1981)

Multi-agency management of cases of child abuse is often remarkably similar to the sequence of events which followed Chicken Licken's unfortunate initial assessment, and the spiralling collaboration in his treatment plan by a succession of colleagues, none of whom cared to question the initial hypothesis. Families and agencies frequently become *stuck* in repetitive sequences of behaviour, often applying more and more 'solutions' without stopping and taking time to re-examine the *problem*, and each party's role in it. In an attempt to deal with these issues we developed network meetings as a forum for the professionals and the family together to re-examine the helping process. Network meetings are therapeutic meetings between the family, the significant agencies involved with them, and a neutral convenor.

The convenor focuses on the family as leaders of and responsible for the problem-solving network. Thus, instead of being worked on by others, the family are encouraged to take responsibility and to question their dependence on professionals. The family are treated as *experts on themselves*.

The network meeting will follow a defined but flexible pattern. The family will be invited to sit at the head of a horseshoe-shaped seating arrangement, with their professionals extending from them. The convenor will begin the meeting by asking each person in turn to introduce him or herself, and will then ask each professional in turn to state what their job is. It is astonishing how difficult many professionals find it to define their jobs concisely. This is often a reflection of the fact that in many 'stuck' inter-agency systems, various professionals have drifted wildly out of role. The second round enquires of each professional, 'What is your problem in helping this family?'; and of the family, 'What are the problems for which you need help?'

This question focuses on the area of professional honesty, and again it is often remarkable the extent to which professionals of all disciplines are unable to tell families exactly what they are worried about. A failure to clarify problems in this verbal round may lead the convenor to follow with further questions such as 'What is your second biggest problem?' or 'What solutions have you tried?' This enables the network to establish a hierarchy of problems, and distinguishes between the perceptions of each professional and the family members. In some network meetings, one of the predominant impressions is of a multi-disciplinary professional group simultaneously attempting to operationalize 'solutions' without an adequately defined or agreed view of the 'problem'.

The *problem* round also releases information as to who is most worried: levels of debilitating anxiety and enmeshment can be observed by the whole group. *How* people define a problem is also important, for example in respect of how much jargon the professionals use and how they may mystify rather than clarify matters to the family. This round may also bring into the open the common experience of families who are subject to a number of professionals simultaneously attempting to influence them with *conflicting therapeutic models*. Often the contrast in therapeutic models is so great that at best they cancel one another out, and at worst they confuse and intensify pathological family dynamics.

After these verbal rounds, the convenor will call on the family (both parents separately if time allows) to produce a sculpt of their perception of themselves and the professionals around them. Through posture, gesture, and contact the sculpt becomes a physical representation of all the relationships within the family–agency system. The professionals are made dramatically aware of how the family perceives what they are attempting to do. This may involve quite honest feedback from clients, as when one mother sculpted the symbolic gesture of her social worker as being 'just one big mouth'.

Other significant lessons for professionals may emerge when a parent struggles to put several workers standing on the same spot, unable to differentiate between their roles and actions. Clients may also demonstrate that they are acutely sensitive to conflicts and rivalries between their various professionals; they may even be encouraged by the convenor to show that they enjoy fuelling such conflicts.

After the sculpting, the network meetings will move into its final phase which involves work on yet another mechanism of communication. All members are given paper and pens, the professionals being asked to write concisely the answer to two questions:

A. What do you *have* to do as part of your statutory or professional responsibility with this family? B. What are you prepared to *offer* this family? The family are asked to give written answers to the question: 'What are you prepared to do for yourselves?'

The professionals are asked to present their written statements to the parents. The parents are asked to consider both sets of answers, and to indicate which of the professional roles and offers they wish to accept. They may refuse them all (presuming that no statutory order exists on the children), accept them all, or select some and decline others. One major consequence is that perhaps for the first time the family is placed in the position of being able clearly and specifically to 'hire and fire' its helpers. Indeed, professionals who had previously considered themselves to be an essential part of the family's survival may find themselves 'sacked' by parents who declare previously concealed resentment at their dependence on such 'support'.

In cases where there is a statutory child care order in force, the social worker will be asked by the convenor to clarify exactly what is required from the family under the terms of the order. The social worker will be encouraged to be specific, and to state what action he or she will take if the family does not comply. Similarly the parents will be asked to state whether they accept these conditions or not, and if not whether they are now aware of the consequences which will follow.

Network meetings end with the family having understood the written offers and clarified which of their professional relationships they wish to continue and which they wish to terminate. Professional roles and responsibilities have become clear, as has the family's own responsibility for working towards desired changes. The statutory responsibilities of each professional have been outlined, and the parents are specifically aware of what is expected of them, and what help is available.

In 80 per cent of the network meetings subsequent work with the family showed a marked change of direction, with agencies either closing cases which had been open for several years, or taking legal action to protect the children and to place the relationship with the family on a formal assessment footing. In several cases the professional group became acutely aware of the basic unviability of the family, and the degree to which children were neglected and in physical danger. In several other cases, long histories of unbroken social work 'support' came to an end (in one case a family had had social workers continuously for twenty years), and the families became able to function adequately without perpetual multi-agency involvement.

The effective use of a network meeting where the case-conference system had become 'stuck' in respect of a baby at acute risk, is described in Chapter 6.

Child protection

Investigations

It is vital for the prevention of serious cases of child abuse, and the avoidance of patterns of repeated injury, that suspicious incidents, injuries, and allegations of abuse are thoroughly and promptly investigated. No matter how efficiently co-ordinated and harmonious the inter-agency system, at the point of crisis intervention the safety of many children will depend on appropriate, prompt, and decisive action being taken by the social worker responsible for investigating an allegation of child abuse.

An emphasis on a thorough investigation of all suspicious injuries, even the most minor, has the effect of improving general professional concern about the welfare of children. Investigations begin with concerns expressed about a child. Such concerns may arise from direct observation of a suspicious injury, or may develop from information received from another party – for example a member of the public, a neighbour, or an extended-family member. Local inter-agency child abuse procedures will make clear who does what during an investigation, but the steps required to afford appropriate protection to the child remain standard:

1. Whoever is first alerted should wherever possible seek consultation with a designated manager, or a colleague. Families in which abuse occurs are very powerful, and professionals are likely to need help. The abuse of a child can bring out feelings that may frighten and astonish, and in doing so can overwhelm and disable practitioners. It is important for feelings of revulsion, anger, guilt, and – worse of all – disbelief to be

brought into the open and shared. Such reactions can seriously distort professional perceptions and responses.

2. Obtain additional information. Contact other professionals and agencies who have contact with the child and his or her family. Enquire as to past or current concerns of the school, nursery, health visitor, and other agencies known to be involved.

3. *See the child.* This is an absolute requirement following any allegation of ill-treatment or neglect. On receipt of such a referral, efforts to see the child should begin immediately, and the child should be seen in any event within twenty-four hours. If a social worker for reasons of pressure of work cannot achieve this, then senior management of the agency should immediately be informed.

It may be that the investigation begins with a knock on an unknown family's door, followed by an explanation from the worker concerned about who he or she is and the reason for the visit. Regardless of the response from the adults, the primary task remains that of *seeing the child*. If entry to the premises is prevented, and access to the child denied, then immediate police assistance is indicated. Such occasions are very exceptional. Most members of the public are aware that such investigations are required when complaints are received, and will usually accept the intrusion with degrees of distress or passive hostility.

A careful note should be made of the child's condition, any observations of visible injuries, together with the parents' account of how they occurred. Observations are also important of the child's emotional state and behaviour to his or her parents and the worker. Following any allegation of injury or neglect, *seeing the child* means seeing under the child's clothing. It is *not* sufficient only to establish that there are no bruises or injuries to the face, legs, and arms. This is especially so with allegations of neglect – once undressed a child who when clothed had not appeared abnormal may stand out as significantly skinny or wasted.

Observed injuries

Whenever injuries and bruises are observed, an explanation should be sought from the parents or care-takers and, if old enough, from the child. The colour of bruises is highly significant, and provide a rough guide to the age of the injury. Colour of bruising changes from black to purple, to brown, to green, then to yellow. Most bruises tend to disappear in three to four weeks, and each colour change may take about one week. Pressure bruises from finger marks are always flush with the skin, and the skin is not broken. In contrast, blows to the skin with a hard object usually cause swelling, and may rupture the skin. The outline of the object used may also be visible, for example a slipper, stick, or belt.

When such bruises and marks are discovered it is essential that the child be examined by a doctor who is experienced in the medical aspects of child abuse. Doctors who rarely encounter child abuse may miss very significant signs. Where there is uncertainty about the cause of an injury, this should be regarded as very suspicious if one of the factors identified by Gregg (1968) apply:

'1. Where there is a history of accident, do the details of the accident adequately explain the location and extent of the injuries?
2. If the child is supposed to have contributed to the accident through its own motor activity, is the alleged activity consistent with its developmental level?
3. Are there significant discrepancies in the story of the accident as reported by various responsible adults?
4. Where there is more than one injury and where these have occurred at distinctly different times, can each be adequately explained?'

(Gregg 1968: 720–25)

Professionals should also be suspicious even when the injury could conceivably have been caused in the manner described, if parental attitudes and history indicate additional cause for concern.

Medical examination

In all cases where there is any suspicion that the observed injury has been inflicted, the professional involved should ensure that the child receives a prompt medical examination, preferably by a doctor experienced in child abuse. Such an examination is essential, regardless of the severity of the injury, because:

1. There may be evidence of previous undiagnosed injuries – for example healed fractures;
2. There may be more serious injuries which require specialist diagnosis and treatment;
3. There may be underlying medical conditions to apparently inflicted injuries – for example brittle bones or blood disorders;
4. A medical opinion may be required for any legal proceedings which may follow to protect the child.

When a firm diagnosis of inflicted injury has been made and the child requires treatment, or when it is not safe for him or her to return home, it is usually appropriate for the paediatric unit to be used as the place of safety, pending the child's transfer to a suitable foster home.

Informing the police

In Britain, there is no legal obligation to report cases of child abuse to the police, unless death has occurred. However, in most areas, there will be an understanding with the police regarding the sorts of cases which they expect to be referred to them because of the criminal aspect of the assault. For example, the Rochdale multi-disciplinary guidelines state: 'In the case of serious multiple injuries immediate referral to the police should be made.'

Like other agencies, all police forces reserve the right to take action even if the agreement of other agencies is not forthcoming. However, in our experience it is most unusual for a serious disagreement about police investigation of an incident of child abuse to occur. Police representation at all child abuse case-conferences has enabled positive relationships with the police to be formed, and the police presence is seen as a valuable part of the inter-disciplinary management of child abuse.

Protecting the child

Following medical confirmation of an inflicted injury, the key question is whether it is safe and appropriate for the child to return home or whether a protective order is necessary. The seriousness of the injury is not in itself a guide, because although it is unlikely that a seriously injured child would be allowed home immediately, moderate and minor injuries can also reflect very dangerous family dynamics. The attitudes of the parents, and the emotional state of the child, will be crucial factors. Also of importance will be the initial assessment of both the seriousness of the problems within the family and the parents' responses to offers of appropriate help.

Certainly, where there is continuing denial of responsibility for the injury, or where parental attitudes remain evasive, secretive, and devious, a place of safety order for the child is strongly indicated. *The position of any siblings must also be reviewed.* The stance of *child protection* in such situations of initial uncertainty means assuming that the siblings are at as great a risk as the victim – *not* that they are at less risk because they were not harmed. In many situations the *only safe* course is to remove the uninjured siblings from home, also on the basis of a place of safety order, until a clearer initial assessment of the family can be made.

For all intervention with child-abusing families, it is important to deal with the crucial protection issues before attempting to assess and provide treatment for the underlying difficulties. The maxim of 'protection before therapy' demands a thorough understanding and constructive use of child care legislation.

CHAPTER 3

Legal context

It was noted in Chapter 1 that the last century has seen a rapid development of legislation intended to protect and promote the physical well-being of children. The major tension in child-protective legislation has offset the desire to afford necessary protection to children suffering from or at risk of abuse against the need to respect parental rights and responsibilities, and, others would add, the need to avoid undue interference by the state in family life.

Such tensions are as alive today as ever, and a range of influential pressure groups exist to promote particular interests. Such groups play a predominantly helpful role as they develop expertise in presenting the dilemmas and difficulties affecting their particular interest, and in pushing for change in child care legislation and practice which, in England and Wales, are incredibly complex. Reform of the entire child care legal system in England and Wales is long overdue, as the current combinations of courts and criteria are confusing, if not largely incomprehensible, to many professionals and families alike.

In the meantime it is essential that practitioners gain a good understanding of current legislation, together with an awareness of the possibilities it does present for constructive statutory intervention to protect children and to provide a context for the promotion of change in their families. This chapter will describe and illustrate the different types of child-protective legal proceedings available in England and Wales which provide a statutory *mandate* for subsequent assessment and therapeutic work with the child and the family. Chapter 4 focuses on the therapeutic potential of statutory mandates; this chapter concentrates on how to obtain them.

Immediate protection of children

Legal powers to protect children are vested in the police, local authorities (through the social services department), and the NSPCC. These three agencies are authorized to institute care proceedings through a juvenile court. In addition, each of these agencies is authorized to obtain a *place of safety order* on a child where there is 'reasonable cause to believe' that one (or more) of the criteria for bringing care proceedings are met (see pp. 53–4). For the social services department and the NSPCC the mechanism for obtaining a place of safety order is by personal application to a magistrate, who is empowered to grant an order for a maximum period of twenty-eight days. Within this period, if the cause for concern remains, the application must be brought before a bench of the juvenile court where an *interim care order* may be granted for a further period of twenty-eight days if the court is satisfied that there continues to be reasonable cause for concern that such criteria have been or are being met.

It is important to note that the procedure for the police to obtain a place of safety order is quite different. The police can effect such an order without application to a magistrate on the authority of a senior police officer (of inspector rank or above) who personally signs the application. Police place of safety orders last for eight days only. Although in principle it is difficult to argue with the desirability of involving the judicial process in emergency steps to protect children, many night-duty social workers and NSPCC officers can reflect upon the value of police place of safety orders in the rare circumstances in which they are called for.

Although in practice it is the local authorities, the NSPCC, and the police who obtain place of safety orders, it is less commonly known that *any* individual can apply to a magistrate for a child to be detained and taken to a place of safety.

Search and entry warrants

Section 40 of the Children and Young Persons Act, 1933, provides a procedure for the issuing of a warrant allowing the police to enter premises, by force if necessary, to search for a child thought to be at risk, and then to remove him or her to a place of safety. Magistrates may issue such warrants on application (by the local authority or the NSPCC), if they are satisfied that there is reasonable cause to suspect: (1) that the child is the victim of an assault, ill-treatment, or neglect likely to cause unnecessary suffering or injury to health; or (2) that any offence mentioned in the First Schedule to this Act has been or is being committed in respect of the child or young person. Schedule 1 offences are described on pp. 57–8.

Child-protective legislation

There are three major types of legal proceedings through which a local authority may gain care and control over a child in place of the child's parents. These are through *care proceedings*, *wardship applications*, and *parental rights resolutions*. Each procedure will be described in turn with particular focus on the relevance to child abuse.

Care proceedings

Care proceedings are brought under Section 1 of the Children and Young Persons Act, 1969. The proceedings are in two stages, which are commonly known as the 'proof' stage and the 'report' stage. At the proof stage when oral evidence only is admissible (apart from written medical evidence as to a person's physical or mental condition), the court must be satisfied that one or more of the *primary conditions* in Section 1(2) are applicable *and* the child is in need of care and control which he or she is unlikely to receive unless the court makes an order.

Primary grounds for care proceedings

'(a) his proper development is being avoidably prevented or neglected or his health is being avoidably impaired or neglected or he is being ill-treated; or

(b) it is probable that the condition set out in the preceding paragraph will be satisfied in his case, having regard to the fact that the court or another court has found that that condition is or was satisfied in the case of another child or young person who is or was a member of the household to which he belongs; or (bb) it is probable that the conditions set out in paragraph (a) of the sub-section will be satisfied in his case, having regard to the fact that a person who has been convicted of an offence mentioned in Schedule 1 of the Act of 1933, including a person convicted of such an offence on whose conviction for the offence an order was made under Part 1 of the Powers of Criminal Courts Act, 1973, placing him on probation or discharging him absolutely or conditionally is, or may become, a member of the same household as the child or young person; or

(c) he is exposed to moral danger; or

(d) he is beyond the control of his parent or guardian; or

(e) he is of compulsory school age within the meaning of the Education Act of 1944, and is not receiving efficient full-time education suitable to his age, ability, and aptitude; or

(f) he is guilty of an offence, excluding homicide.'

At the proof stage the court must be satisfied on the *balance of probabilities* that one or more of these primary conditions have been proved. It is important to note the level of evidence required: care proceedings are civil proceedings, therefore the evidence must be on the 'balance of probabilities' rather than the more stringent 'beyond reasonable doubt' required in criminal proceedings.

Once the court is satisfied that a primary ground has been proved, it will consider the 'care and control' test to determine whether an order needs to be made in respect of the child. Whilst each primary condition relates to a specific and relatively narrow aspect of the child's situation and behaviour, the care and control test is much more general and the court will consider the likely future course of events if an order is or is not made. Care is defined as protection and guidance, and control as discipline. The issue is not whether the parents are doing as well as might be expected considering their situation, but whether, in the light of all the circumstances, what form of order, if any, is required for the child to receive the necessary care and control.

Only when both stages have been completed and the court is satisfied that an order of some sort is required will the proceedings move to the report stage at which written reports are provided with recommendations to the court as to what type of order it should make.

Before we examine the types of order open to the court at this stage, it will be useful to look in more detail at Sub-sections (a) to (c) and to consider how they may be interpreted in practice. It is unlikely that Sub-sections (d) to (f) would comprise the primary ground for an application following child abuse.

Sub-section (a) reads 'his proper development is being avoidably prevented or neglected or his health is being avoidably impaired or neglected or he is being ill-treated'.

This clause covers a large number of applications in respect of children who have suffered inflicted injury or injuries; children whose physical and emotional development is significantly adversely affected; and children who are being neglected. Medical evidence will often be important to establish that the impaired development or poor health is *avoidable*, and that the parents in many cases have failed to co-operate with necessary treatment or advice. 'Before and after' medical evidence regarding the progress that the child has made after being taken into care is often highly significant in demonstrating the phenomenon of growth spurts which young children often make while in hospital or in foster care. Such rapid increases in growth and weight in short periods away from home are often crucial in establishing that the type of care the child has received has determined his or her growth or lack of it.

The general interpretation of this sub-section relates to existing events, not to speculation about any future harm the child might come to, no matter how imminent.

However, in a judgment on interpretation of this sub-section in 1981 it was established that 'proper development' applies equally to the emotional development of the child, and that proceedings may be brought in respect of the child's probable future development (F. v. Suffolk CC (1981)). It was also established in the same judgment that an experienced social worker or health visitor can claim expert witness status in such proceedings, although this claim may be challenged by other parties.

For cases of ill-treatment and injury, particularly where there is a conflict over how the injury occurred, it is usually necessary to bring the evidence of a paediatrician to state whether or not the explanations given are credible. Paediatric evidence is usually firmer in saying how an injury did *not* occur, than specific as to how it did occur. Such evidence is vital, however, and all children suffering from suspected abuse should ideally have a thorough paediatric examination, usually including an X-ray skeletal survey. Skeletal surveys may on occasion reveal previous healed fractures.

It is common in cases of physical abuse for there to be discrepant explanations as to how a child came to be injured, and a series of 'accidental' events may be outlined. Even in cases of severe injury, police enquiries may fail to discover who was responsible when met by parents and other family members who collude to maintain a 'cover' story. Unless a person admits causing such an injury, or there is some corroborative evidence to establish a person's responsibility, then criminal charges cannot be brought.

For care proceedings following ill-treatment, however, it is not necessary to prove *who* was responsible for injuring the child, only that the child has suffered an inflicted injury.

Sub-section (b) reads

'it is probable that the condition set out in the preceding paragraph will be satisfied in his case, having regard to the fact that the court or another court has found that that condition is or was satisfied in the case of another child or young person who is or was a member of the household to which he belongs'.

The 'same household' clause enables an application to be made in respect of any other children who live with the same care-takers at the same time as or subsequently to a child found by a court to have suffered avoidable impaired development, ill-treatment, or neglect. This clause enables protective orders to be made on the *siblings* of such children if they are thought to be at risk, even if they themselves have not as yet suffered in such a way. Additionally the clause provides grounds for proceedings in respect of any future children those parents may have – including taking babies into care at birth on the authority of a place of safety order.

When one child has been harmed and the court has heard an application under Sub-section (a) in respect of him or her, and this has been found proved, it is not uncommon for an application under Sub-section (b) to be heard in respect of the other children in the household. As part of such proceedings the court will wish to hear evidence that the parental omissions or commissions which gave rise to the difficulties with the injured child are also apparent or likely to occur with the siblings.

The public inquiry report into the case of John Auckland (Auckland 1975) demonstrated that siblings of abused children require protection from future abuse. Having served a prison sentence for the manslaughter of one of his children, John Auckland was allowed to care for his other children following his release, and subsequently was responsible for another death.

Sub-section (bb)

'it is probable that the conditions set out in paragraph (a) of the sub-section will be satisfied in his case, having regard to the fact that a person who has been convicted of an offence mentioned in Schedule 1 of the Act of 1933, including a person convicted of such an offence on whose conviction for the offence an order was made under Part 1 of the Powers of Criminal Courts Act, 1973, placing him on probation or discharging him absolutely or conditionally is, or may become, a member of the same household as the child or young person'.

The 'Schedule 1' clause was added to the care proceedings criteria in 1975 following the DHSS (Department of Health and Social Security) response to points made in the Auckland inquiry report. It was clarified that Sub-section (b) only applied to other children ill-treated in the same household as the child presently alleged to be at risk of ill-treatment. Sub-section (bb) was introduced to cover children at risk from a member of the household who was previously the member of a different household where a child was ill-treated.

Consequently, the 'Schedule 1 Offence' clause allows proceedings to be brought for any child who is, or may become, a member of a household of a person convicted of such an offence. This applies both when the offender joins the child's household and when the child joins the offender's household.

Schedule 1 offences are detailed in the Children and Young Persons Act of 1933 and are as follows: murder, manslaughter, infanticide; abandoning, child stealing, assault; cruelty, allowing persons between 4 years and 16 years to be in brothels; begging, dangerous performance by children; procurement by threat, false pretences, or drugs; intercourse with a girl under 16 years; intercourse with a defective; incest, indecency between men, buggery; indecent assault, assault with intent to commit buggery; abduction, causing prostitution; any attempt to commit the above;

any other offence involving bodily injury to a child or young person.

The introduction of the 'Schedule 1 clause' was a response to concern about situations where offenders with a history of serious offences against children were found to be involved subsequently in further child abuse. Most social workers know of men with records of violence against children who seem to hang around households of single mothers, bringing fear, if not further violence, in their wake. In addition, some young mothers seem particularly liable to allow or even encourage such characters to enter their homes, with little regard to the physical or emotional consequences to their children.

The clause is of value in that it allows local authorities to intervene to prevent children from remaining in the care of persons with a wide range of convictions for offences against children, if it is considered – and this is not an automatic assumption – that they continue to present a risk. As with Sub-section (b), this clause also applies to parents who have had all their children removed from them following conviction for serious injury or manslaughter, when another pregnancy occurs.

Following conviction for a serious Schedule 1 offence, it is important that parents be made aware of the implications in respect of future children they may have. It has been our experience that some parents convicted of manslaughter have conceived another child on release from prison without being aware of the legislation which allows such a child to be removed from them. Parents in this position should be made aware of the need to discuss with the local authority the likely reaction to such a pregnancy *before* it occurs.

It is important to note that as from 15 August, 1983 (by virtue of the Health and Social Services and Social Security Adjudications Act, 1983), Schedule 1 offenders sentenced to probation orders, or absolute or conditional discharges, are counted as having been convicted for the purposes of care proceedings. Previously they were excluded. Similarly, for the purposes of care proceedings, such convictions are never spent (Section 7, Rehabilitation of Offenders Act, 1974).

Sub-section (c) reads 'he is exposed to moral danger'.

As in all of the sub-sections, 'he' is to be read as including 'she'. This section is potentially very wide, and definition is dependent on the court's interpretation of morality. In the context of child abuse within the family the clause covers the whole spectrum of sexual abuse, whether the child is actively involved, a passive victim, or an onlooker at adult sexual activity. Outside the family, the sub-section would cover children engaged in unlawful or promiscuous sexual activity such as prostitution.

The crucial issue is whether the acts, incidents, and environment to which a child is subjected are damaging to that child. The sub-section does not aim to punish parents for an unorthodox sexual life-style: the issue is not the life-style of the parents but whether or not this is damaging to the child. Specifically, parental prostitution or homosexuality do not in themselves constitute 'moral danger' to the child – the test is the effect on the child.

As all agencies involved in the protection of children become increasingly aware of the incidence and damaging emotional effects of incest, the 'moral danger' clause is likely to become of great significance as the basis for protection of victims and siblings. In many cases of sexual abuse it is not possible for the police to secure a conviction against the perpetrator, either for lack of corroborative evidence or because the victim withdraws a (true) allegation. Cases of sexual abuse, as much as serious physical abuse, require a firm legal mandate on which to base assessment and treatment programmes. The authors' work on sexual abuse is described elsewhere (Dale *et al.*, 1986).

Care proceedings: The report stage

Having satisfied itself that the conditions of one or more of the criteria described have been met, *and* that the child is in need of care and control which he or she is unlikely to receive without an order being made, the court will consider written reports and hear further evidence if necessary to determine what type of order would be in the child's best interests. Although there is no requirement for the local authority to explain how it intends to manage whatever order the court decides to make, it is good practice for the professional social worker involved with the family to explain his or her plan for the future and how the making of a particular order will fit with this.

At the report stage all other parties have the opportunity to oppose the type of order being recommended by the local authority; often parents argue for a supervision order rather than a care order. There are five types of order which a juvenile court may make at the conclusion of care proceedings. These are:

1. An order requiring the child's parent to enter into recognizance to take proper care of him and exercise proper control over him.

2. A supervision order placing the child under the supervision of the local authority, or in certain circumstances a probation officer.

3. A care order committing the child to the care of the local authority, which remains in effect until the child is 18 or until the order is revoked by the court.

4. & 5. Hospital and guardianship orders can be made when a court has evidence that the child's mental condition warrants detention in a specified hospital, or placement under the guardianship of the local health authority.

Only two of these dispositions are of any real significance for care proceedings following child abuse: care orders and supervision orders.

Care orders

Care orders give the local authority power to determine where and with whom a child shall live until he or she attains the age of eighteen. In effect, all the powers and duties of the parents are transferred to the local authority, and in planning and providing for such children the authority must further their best interests and afford them the opportunity for proper development. A juvenile court cannot instruct or supervise the local authority in the exercise of its powers over a child subject to a care order. However, the local authority has a statutory duty to hold a formal review of the child's progress in care every six months, under the chairmanship of a senior manager who preferably has no direct involvement in the case. Specific plans for the child's future should be stated.

In terms of social work practice, most social services departments and child care practitioners would now subscribe to the principle of *permanency planning* for children in care; that is, they should plan either for the child to return home as soon as possible or for a permanent placement in a substitute family to be found. Hopefully, as such practices take effect, considerably fewer children on care orders will be allowed to 'drift' in care through multiple placements without firm plans for their future. Most experienced social workers will be familiar with inheriting as clients young adults who spent chaotic and disjointed childhoods in the 'care' of a local authority which made no consistent or permanent plans for them. It is a peculiarly damaging process.

This book demonstrates the use of care orders to provide the legal *mandate* for an assessment and treatment programme to determine whether children removed from home following child abuse can return to the care of their parents, or whether alternative permanent substitute parents are required. The work described demonstrates the usefulness of care orders even when children are quickly returned 'home on trial' to their parents. Returning children 'home on trial' on care orders allows the local authority to stipulate that their remaining with their parents is dependent on conditions and specific standards of parenting, as well as co-operation with agencies.

Care orders are not magical potions which in themselves create significant changes in families. The potential for change lies in the therapeutic opportunities provided by a firm statutory mandate. As part of this process in a rehabilitation phase, children will be returned 'home on trial' to the day-to-day care of their parents. It is good social work practice for children 'home on trial' to be visited at home by the social worker at least as frequently as they would be under the Boarding-out Regulations. The Boarding-out of Children Regulations, 1955, specify as a legal requirement the frequency with which a local authority must visit a child in care in a foster home. In addition to a visit within one month of the placement, a child under five years of age must be visited every six weeks for the first two years, and every three months subsequently. A child over the age of five must be visited every two months for the first two years, and then every three months.

It is a requirement of the Boarding-out Regulations that the child must be actually *seen* on such visits. The same principle should hold for children 'home on trial' on care orders, and on such visits the child's bedroom should be inspected. The use of care orders for rehabilitation following child abuse is illustrated in Chapter 8.

Parties to care proceedings

In recent years there have been several changes in the law

governing care proceedings. A major change occurred in 1984: from 27 May, courts were given new powers, in a wide range of proceedings affecting children, to appoint a guardian *ad litem* to safeguard the interests of the child in the proceedings. For many years prior to this it was not possible for parents to obtain legal aid for a solicitor to represent their case to the court, and only the *child* (who could be legally aided) and the *applicant* (the local authority or the NSPCC) were parties to the proceedings. This was widely felt to be an unsatisfactory state of affairs, and many solicitors representing children in such proceedings found themselves more or less taking instructions from the parents, and representing the parental point of view. This was equally unsatisfactory, because of the likelihood of a conflict of interest between the parents and the child. The introduction of legal aid for parents as well as children, and the role of the guardian *ad litem*, have to a large extent remedied many of these problems.

The guardian *ad litem* is an experienced, practising social worker appointed to a panel which each local authority is required to maintain. In most areas, groups of local authorities join together to form a combined panel; for example Rochdale, Oldham, and Bury have a shared panel of guardians *ad litem*. Social workers from statutory and voluntary agencies in each area act as guardian *ad litem* for cases in the other two local authority areas.

The guardian *ad litem* is an officer of the court, and in this capacity acts independently of his employing agency. His statutory function is to safeguard the interests of the child. He will be expected to interview all parties involved in the proceedings (i.e. all the relevant agencies, the parents, and the child), and to assess and appraise not only the problems within the family, but also the work of the professionals involved with the case. A detailed report will be provided for the court, in which the guardian *ad litem* will outline the options open to the court, and will advise on the basis of his expert opinion what course is in the child's best long-term interest.

As part of this role, the guardian *ad litem* (who instructs the child's solicitor) will play a major role in the court proceedings; through his solicitor calling and cross-examining witnesses. At the conclusion of care proceedings, the guardian can *appeal* against a decision of the juvenile court if he feels the court has not acted in the child's interests. In fact in cases where a guardian *ad litem* has been appointed, it is *only* the guardian who can appeal against such a *decision* of the juvenile court, this right not being afforded to the parents or the local authority. Where there has not been a guardian *ad litem* in proceedings, the parents remain able to lodge an appeal – on behalf of the child – against a juvenile court decision.

It should be noted that appeals on matters of law or procedure may be brought by any party to the proceedings, or by any person aggrieved by the manner in which the proceedings have been conducted in the juvenile court. Such appeals are usually brought to the Divisional Court. Although local authorities cannot formally appeal against a decision of a juvenile court, a practice has been used increasingly in recent years whereby an application is made by the local authority to the High Court to make a child a *ward of court* when it is considered that the juvenile court has not acted to protect the interests – and particularly the safety – of a child. This process is described in more detail later in this chapter.

If the guardian *ad litem* lodges an appeal on the child's behalf against a decision of the juvenile court, the original case is reheard in the Crown Court by a judge and two magistrates.

Applications to revoke care orders

A person subject to a care order, his or her parent(s), or the local authority concerned may apply to the juvenile court for the discharge of the order. The court can decide to discharge the order and substitute a supervision order, discharge the order completely, or refuse the application. If the application is refused, no further application to discharge the order can be made for the next three months. In deciding whether a discharge or variation of the order would be appropriate, the court will need to hear evidence about the circumstances in which the order was made in order to assess the changes which have occurred. The court may appoint a guardian *ad litem* to help it to come to a decision.

Supervision orders

Supervision orders may be made for a period of between one and three years, and require the local authority to appoint a person (usually the area team social worker) to 'advise, assist and befriend' the child. Supervision orders do not confer a right of entry into the child's home, nor do they contain any stipulation as to where, or with whom, the child should live. Parental rights are retained in full by the parents.

Following a recommendation of the Maria Colwell inquiry, from 1976 onwards it became possible to have a clause inserted in supervision orders that the supervised person may be medically examined at the requirement of the supervisor.

Many social workers feel that supervision orders following child abuse are inadequate as they contain few 'teeth' to require of parents that the care of the child should improve. In many cases, supervision orders bring little change in the social worker's relationships with a family, and patterns of unproductive home visiting which may have been in operation before the child was abused merely continue on a more formal footing.

Supervision orders may be used in a somewhat different way, however. After such an order is made, the local authority has a legal responsibility to ensure that the parents' care of the child is adequate. It is then quite appropriate for the social worker to specify to the parents exactly what is required of them in terms of improvements in their care of the child, and in respect of their co-operation with the helping and supervisory agencies. It is valuable to specify these matters in writing to the parents at an early stage, and to include a specific offer of therapeutic help to assist them in working towards the required changes.

Often the offer of a specific structure of therapeutic work for parents is quite different from any of the other approaches made to them in the past by social workers and other professionals, and as such increases their responsibility to use such offers productively. If parental co-operation does not result from such a specific statement of concern and offer of a therapeutic programme, and little in the child's life appears to be changing, then it is open to the local authority to bring the matter quickly back to the juvenile court.

When parents fail to co-operate with the reasonable requirements of a supervisor, and the child is felt to remain at risk of further abuse, an application can be made by the local authority for the supervision order to be revoked and a *care order* substituted. Such proceedings do not need to go back over the original *primary* ground for the application, only to hear fresh evidence that the original order is not adequate to afford the child sufficient care and control.

Following such an application the court will almost certainly wish to have a report from a guardian *ad litem*, and in the meantime will need to decide whether the child should remain on the supervision order, or whether an interim care order should be granted (the child being taken into care pending the outcome of the proceedings). In some cases the child on a supervision order will have been taken into care on a place of safety order; the court will then usually hear a request from the local authority for an interim care order.

Wardship applications

Wardship applications to the Family Division of the High Court can be made by way of originating summons by any interested party to request that a child be made a ward of court (Supreme Court Act, 1981). In such an application it is necessary to demonstrate cause for concern about any events which may have befallen or may befall a child. Wardship proceedings adjudicate solely on the basis of 'the best interests of the child', and there is no requirement to prove specific conditions or criteria.

The High Court has far greater authority and scope to respond to a wider range of concerns than does the juvenile court. When a child is made a ward of court, the court *directs* the living situation of the child which may then not be changed without reference back to the court. Orders made under wardship proceedings can include care orders and supervision orders to the local authority; placement with specified adults; and a range of other conditions which the court may impose in the interests of the child.

As in juvenile court care proceedings, the High Court will often require an independent report to assist it; and in wardship proceedings the Official Solicitor may be appointed to act as guardian *ad litem* for the child. The local authority panels of guardians *ad litem* are not used in wardship cases.

Many local authorities are using wardship proceedings increasingly in child-protective work, partly because of a measure of dissatisfaction with the operation of juvenile court care proceedings. In particular, local authorities are more frequently taking immediate recourse to a wardship application as an indirect means of 'appealing' against a juvenile court's decision to discharge a care order, or where any other decision of the juvenile court is felt to be insufficient to afford the necessary degree of protection to a child. In such cases the refusal by a juvenile court to grant a care order implies that a child in care on an interim care order should immediately be returned home.

By making an immediate wardship application, the local authority can retain the child in care until specific instructions are given by a High Court judge. As already noted, the High Court will take into account a far wider view of the child's interests than the juvenile court is empowered to do. It is for this reason that wardship is also being used by local authorities to secure a child's compulsory admission to care where insufficient grounds exist to bring care proceedings. In such cases it is likely that the local authority will present evidence of serious concern about some event which threatens to affect the child.

As with care proceedings, one possible outcome of a wardship application is that in effect the local authority can be given parental rights over a child. The *discretion* for the local authority to exercise that responsibility, however, is far more limited than that given by a care order following care proceedings. If children are made wards of court, then every decision which materially affects them, for example where they should live, has to be referred back to the court for guidance. There is no reason, in the context of good professional practice, why firm plans for a permanent placement of a child – either back with the natural family or, if this is not possible, with a permanent substitute family – should not follow and be supported by the court.

Parental rights resolutions

The third major route for a local authority to gain care and control of a child applies only to children who are already in voluntary care. The Child Care Act, 1980 (Section 2), outlines the grounds on which a local authority has a duty to receive a child under the age of seventeen into care. These are that the child has no parent or guardian, or has been and remains abandoned; or that the parents or guardian are prevented (for whatever reason) from providing for his or her proper accommodation, maintenance, and upbringing. According to the Act, it must also be in the child's best interests to be received into care.

Parents can at any time request the return of children in such *voluntary care*, but the local authority has a duty under the Act to assess whether this would be in the child's best interests. If the local authority considers that this would *not* be so, then the same Act provides a set of criteria which, if fulfilled, allow the local authority to *assume parental rights* over the child. The criteria, as outlined in Section 3 of the act, are as follows:

'(a) both parents are dead and there is no guardian or custodian;
(b) i   the child is abandoned;
    ii   the parent suffers from some permanent disability rendering him incapable of caring for the child;
    iii   the parent has a mental disorder (permanent or not) rendering him unfit to have care of the child;
    iv   the parent is unfit to care for the child because of his habits or mode of life;
    v   the parent has consistently failed to discharge the obligations of a parent without reasonable cause, so as to be unfit to care for the child;
(c) an order is in force relating to one parent of the child or an adult who is (or is likely to become) a member of the household comprising the child and the other parent;
(d) the child has been in care for the whole of the previous three years.'

Assumption of parental rights by a local authority in such circumstances is an administrative action by the social services committee on the basis of a recommendation by its professional staff – the social workers in the department. It is not a judicial action involving any form of court process. The assumption of parental rights remains valid unless the parents formally declare their opposition. When opposition is indicated, the local authority must bring the matter before the juvenile court within fourteen days.

The criteria for the juvenile court to decide whether to uphold or rescind the parental rights resolution are as follows:

'(a) the grounds on which the local authority passed the resolution were made out at the time *and*
(b) there are *still* grounds (but not necessarily the same ones)

at the time of the hearing *and*
(c) the resolution would be in the child's best interests.'

(DHSS 1984: para. 53)

The court has the power, as in care proceedings, to appoint a guardian *ad litem* to safeguard the interests of the child and to assist the court. All parties can appeal to the High Court against the decision of a juvenile court to uphold or rescind a parental rights resolution.

The administrative nature of parental rights resolutions has become subject to increasing criticism by pressure groups supporting 'parents' rights' in recent years. There is a strong lobby arguing that such powers should be removed from the local authority and vested solely in the judicial system. There has also been concern expressed as to how certain of the criteria have been interpreted, notably the 'mode of life' clause, with suggestions that this may be used to discriminate against families with unorthodox life-styles. Defenders of parental rights resolutions point out that in a high proportion of cases the resolutions are passed with the full agreement of the parents, and that it would be inappropriate to subject such families to unnecessary court proceedings.

Other important legislation

Access proceedings under the Child Care Act, 1980

When a child is made subject to a care order following care proceedings, the local authority has a right to terminate or refuse parental access to the child. In practice, the termination of parental access to a child on a care order will usually follow a decision that the child's future will best be served in an alternative permanent family. Under the legislation the local authority has to give formal notice to the parents that their access is either terminated from the date the notice is served on them, or that their request for access is refused. Parents have a right to apply to the juvenile court for an order granting specified access once they have been officially notified of a termination or refusal of access.

No specific grounds or tests apply in such proceedings. The court is required, in reaching its decision to grant, refuse, vary, or discharge an access order, to regard the child's welfare as the paramount consideration. The child's wishes and feelings should be considered, taking into account his or her age and level of understanding. In practice, the court is likely to request the assistance of a guardian *ad litem*, and his report will include an opinion on the local authority's long-term plan for the child.

Refusal or termination of parental access will in many cases be part of the local authority's plan for providing an adoptive home for children in care who cannot be safely rehabilitated to their own parents. Decisions in the juvenile court regarding parental access will be crucial to the feasibility of adoption. In the early stage of the operation of the regulations governing access proceedings (they came into force on 30 January, 1984), there were some cases where decisions of juvenile courts caused confusion for agencies attempting to provide permanent homes for children.

In one such case a juvenile court refused a parental application for the revocation of a care order (following the unsuccessful attempted rehabilitation of a three-year-old child), but in the subsequent access application by the parents, it refused to support the local authority's termination of parental access. Instead, the parents were granted a monthly access order to the child in care. The local authority was left with a three-year-old in a short-term foster placement who could not return home, and who could not be placed with a prospective adoptive family because of the high level of parental contact. The court order in effect placed the child in a situation epitomizing bad child care practice – drifting in care without a permanent plan for the future. The local authority concerned appealed to the High Court against the access order of the juvenile court.

Adoption legislation

The permanent placement of children who cannot return to their natural families and who are subject to care orders following child abuse encounters further legal hurdles after a successful termination of parental access. The traditional next step is for the child's potential adoptive parents to make an application to the County Court (this can also be done through the juvenile court, though it is less common) for an *adoption order* in respect of the child. Potential adoptive parents will be given the go-ahead to make such an application when the local authority responsible for the child is satisfied that the child is appropriately placed with them. Needless to say, a great deal of attention will have been focused on the child and the prospective adoptive family to ensure that this is the right place for the child to be brought up.

The adoption legislation also calls for a guardian *ad litem* to be appointed to represent the child's interests in such applications. Natural parents will be interviewed extensively in respect of their feelings about the plans being made for the child, and to establish whether or not they are in agreement with these. If natural parents are not in agreement with the application for their child to be adopted, the prospective adopters may make an application to the court as part of their adoption application for the *parents' consent to be dispensed with* on the grounds that it is being *unreasonably withheld*; or that the parent has *abandoned, neglected or persistently ill-treated the child*; or has *failed without cause to discharge the obligations of a parent*.

Applications to dispense with parental consent for adoption require considerable scrutiny not only of the behaviour of the child's natural parents and the ways in which they have failed to provide for his or her needs, but also of the actions of the local authority during the period that the child was in its care. At this stage local authorities which have followed all procedures correctly and have documented their good practice and their reasons for concluding that the child requires an adoptive family generally find the court willing to support their plans for the child. Support may less easily be forthcoming when the local authority displays a record of muddled thinking and chaotic administration, which give parents grounds for claiming that the proper procedures were not followed. It is vital for all social workers involved in planning for children in care to pay constant attention to their administrative as well as their therapeutic work.

Freeing for adoption

Section 14(1) of the Children Act, 1975, came into force on 27 May, 1984. It provides for adoption agencies (which include the local authority in addition to voluntary societies offering such services) to apply to the juvenile court for a child to be freed for adoption. This process allows the agency to establish *in advance* of an application by prospective adoptive parents that there will be no legal barriers – such as lack of parental consent – to the eventual making of an adoption order.

The grounds for dispensing with parental consent are essentially the same as those described in traditional adoption applications (p. 70). 'Freeing' procedures enable and encourage local authorities to begin action at an early stage for the permanent placement with alternative families of children who cannot return to their natural families. It allows the most contentious legal proceedings – e.g. the application to dispense with parental consent – to be heard at a much earlier stage than in traditional adoption proceedings. In many cases it lessens the anxiety of potential adoptive parents by dealing with a major obstacle to the eventual making of an adoption order before the child is placed with them.

Developments in adoption planning

Adoption without subsequent contact with natural families has traditionally been seen as the best possible alternative for children who cannot live with their families of origin. It will probably remain the best possible way of promoting the long-term interests and security of very young children. However, other alternatives are available for older children in care, and a great deal of imaginative thinking has been focused on the question of how to provide these children with the necessary security, whilst recognizing that total severance of natural parental contact may not be appropriate.

It is clear from the reports of many adults adopted as children that their knowledge of or fantasies about their families of origin remain very important to them, and that they feel a 'pull' to establish contact with their blood relatives. These feelings may contribute to difficulties between the child and the adopted parents, particularly during adolescence, and an anxious response on the part of the adoptive parents may further exacerbate these difficulties.

A relatively new idea for tackling some of these issues relating to the adoption of not very young children is that of adoption orders which include parental access – so-called 'contact adoption'. Such orders allow for the long-term placement of the child with full transfer of parental rights but with specified occasional contact with the natural parents. As the use of such orders develop, it will be important that the court at all times recognizes the primacy of the child's interests, and that the 'contact' clause is open to review if necessary.

Contact adoption is likely to be of most value where the natural parents do accept that their child requires an alternative family and can consistently explain this view to the child, and where there is no likelihood of their 'sabotaging' the placement. The contact clause in such situations will allow the child a continuous reminder (even if only once or twice a year) that his or her parents are 'all right'; this should diminish the fantasy responsibilities which many older children feel for their parents' welfare.

Even when the child's natural parents are *not* all right, so long as the child is aware of their circumstances to the best of his or her understanding, and is in a secure family environment, the damaging consequences for the child are likely to be minimized.

Custodianship orders

The custodianship provisions of the Children Act, 1975, came into force on 1 December, 1985. The intention behind custodianship orders must be understood in the context of the concerns which lay behind the 1975 Act. A great deal of publicity had been given to several cases in which children who had been placed for long periods of time with foster families (but not adopted) had been moved to other placements against the wishes of their foster parents.

Three groups of people are entitled to apply for a custodianship order in respect of a child: relatives such as grandparents, stepparents, and foster parents. In agreed cases custodianship orders can be granted after a period of time as short as three months for a child who is being cared for within the extended family of his or her natural parents. Custodianship will increasingly give stepparents an equal share of the rights enjoyed by the natural parent, and will replace the now discouraged process of natural parent–stepparent adoption applications.

Foster parents of children who are in the care of the local authority will be able to make a custodianship application after three years of constant care for the same child. In such cases where an order is granted, the child remains in the care of the local authority but cannot be moved to another placement without a further order of the court.

There is currently considerable uncertainty and debate as to the merits of custodianship versus adoption as the best means of securing the permanent placement of older children in care. Concern has been expressed by the British Agencies for Adoption and Fostering (BAAF) that some early legal judgments appeared to discourage the use of adoption to provide security for the older child in care, and to favour instead the legally less contentious process of custodianship.

In such situations custodianship orders are intended to provide long-term security for children for whom adoption is not the answer, and for children whose legal ties with their own families have not been completely broken. As with all new child care legislation, how the provisions operate in practice will be determined by a sequence of court rulings over a considerable period of time.

Child care legal proceedings: Complexity and chaos

Even a relatively brief summary of the child care legislation in operation for the protection of children reveals the almost incomprehensible combinations of Acts, Statutes, and regulations which have developed in a totally piecemeal fashion over the last century. The various professionals and parties involved in such proceedings are in almost unanimous agreement on the need for a complete revision and consolidation of all child care law, and for the creation of a new structure of courts to deal with such cases.

There is widespread dissatisfaction with the *adversarial* nature of the legal proceedings relating to child-protective matters. There is admiration of the Scottish system of *panel* hearings where the atmosphere is more informal, and the emphasis is on conciliation and agreement between the parties.

To meet such criticisms of the system in England and Wales, which fails to meet the needs of children, and is largely incomprehensible to parents and many professionals, proposals for the establishment of family courts have been supported enthusiastically. Family courts would incorporate all the different court procedures described in this chapter, together with others such as all cases relating to divorce and custody proceedings; and would have an emphasis on conciliation instead of the adversarial approach. As part of this a family court welfare service could be established, which would provide independent reports to the court in divorce, care, and adoption cases, and would also provide an official conciliation service. It is significant that the main opposition to the establishment of such a system comes from the Family Bar Association – the barristers' representative body.

Clearly, as the profession dependent on the adversarial approach in court proceedings, barristers are sensitive to the possibility that family courts might diminish their role, and income. Simplified proceedings to afford necessary protection to children in a family court would go a long way to decrease the alienation experienced by participants in the current legal processes, and in all likelihood would lead to a significant reduction overall in legal costs and expenses.

Family courts are long overdue.

CHAPTER 4

Engagement

The work described in this chapter – indeed throughout this book – is based on an assessment and therapeutic model for families whose children have suffered some form of ill-treatment or injury, and have been taken into care on a compulsory child-protection order. The assessment work takes place essentially with *involuntary* clients – parents who are not seeking help of their own free will. This chapter will focus on some ways of attempting to engage such clients in an assessment process, where the goal, in addition to making the right decision for the child's future, is to develop a therapeutic experience for the parents.

Working with involuntary clients in the area of child abuse is often a very emotionally draining experience. It is not suitable for workers who imagine that change occurs simply as a result of their being 'nice' to their clients. It is not for workers who measure their success in terms of the number of Christmas cards they get from their clients. It may be that the number of Christmas cards received from clients is in inverse proportion to the effectiveness of any therapeutic work undertaken. There will be few 'thank yous' in this area of work; this is particularly true of the initial stages described in this chapter. It is important that workers encountering such families, and the crucial decisions which need to be made about them, do so from the basis of a stable and supportive team.

Referrals

By the time the team has its first contact with a family, it is likely that several months will have passed since the traumatic events which culminated in the child's removal into care. The juvenile court process will probably have been slow, with several adjournments, leaving the family and professionals alike dissatisfied with and alienated by the cumbersome legal system.

The team will not begin assessment work with a family until the legal processes have been completed. The policy of not beginning assessments during legal proceedings is crucial if the team is to make maximum use of its *mandate* to undertake the work. The potency of the assessment lies in the team's authority to make recommendations to the local authority about the future placement of the child. An important aspect of the team–family relationship is the family's awareness that working with the team represents their only chance of having their child returned – apart from further court action. The statutory order (usually a care order) provides the mandate for the assessment work. It is essential that the authority of the team be emphasized clearly and specifically at the beginning of the assessment if any therapeutic progress is to be made. This is often a marked contrast to the parents' previous experience with social workers. This clear-cut emphasis on the team's authority creates a level of anxiety and resistance which can be used and channelled therapeutically as a force for change.

In some cases there may be a preliminary contact with a family at the point where the parents have to decide whether to drop further legal action and work with the team, or whether to continue fighting through the courts. This is an important moment. The team takes a neutral stance, not attempting to influence the parents' decision, simply outlining what the assessment will involve. It is important not to minimize the difficulties and the painful areas involved in the assessment, nor to attempt to cajole the parents into beginning work.

The parents are left with a crucial dilemma. One mother who was faced with the decision of accepting a 'mode of life' parental rights resolution and beginning work with the team, or contesting the resolution through the court summed up her dilemma as follows: 'We can't fight you and work with you at the same time . . . I either fight in court against my past being thrown up against me and get angry, or I sit down here with you and look at my past.'

Other referrals follow a somewhat different course. For example some parents consent to the making of a care order after it has been explained to them that they will then be referred to the team for an assessment. In many cases, both contested and uncontested, the local authority will present the referral for assessment as part of its evidence at the report stage as to why a care order is required. In such cases agreed care orders are invariably more satisfactory to all the parties as work can begin immediately, thereby considerably lessening the time children spend in care pending a decision about their future.

Formation of the therapeutic team

A team approach is seen as an absolute requirement in assessment work with child-abusing families. The first decision will be whether the therapeutic team will be a 'staff' team (i.e. comprised of members of the NSPCC team only) or an '*ad hoc*' team (including workers from an outside agency).

Staff teams

There may be a specific reason for using staff only for a particular assessment, perhaps when a case is seen as particularly difficult or in some way politically sensitive. It is usual for three team members to be assigned to a family. Other numbers may be used, for example four workers when the children are of an age to benefit from separate therapeutic work. This is often the case in sexual abuse assessments. Two workers only may form a team on rare occasions, but this is not to be particularly recommended. The dynamics of 'twosomes' with powerful families mean that they are especially liable to run into difficulties.

In general a therapeutic team of three has proved to be the most stable and productive combination. A decision will be taken as to whether there will be two therapists, or a single therapist and two consultants. Either combination has advantages, and internal team issues will very much affect the plan that is reached. We have tended to use co-therapy with families comprising two parents with difficult reputations! On the other hand we would now rarely use two therapists with a single parent.

Initially the co-therapy model was used for all assessment referrals, but as the team developed, a gradual change was made towards teams comprising a single therapist and two consultants. The use of different therapist–consultant structures is important for sustaining learning processes in established teams, and for creating a shared identity in new teams.

Part of the consultant's role is to make a written record of each session, including the planning and de-briefing discussion. The consultant is not a detached therapist, but takes a role which includes focusing on the dynamics of the new system comprising the family and the therapists. The role is less to do with offering 'clever' therapeutic suggestions and alternative ways of proceeding, than with being aware of difficulties in the whole system. For example, he or she will look out for hazards like the therapists and the family getting 'stuck' – going round and round repetitively in circles – and for the problems of conflict avoidance or enmeshment.

Styles of consultancy will vary considerably; each therapeutic team will need to work out a balance which is comfortable and productive for the different personalities and levels of experience of the members. Many therapeutic teams will go through difficult stages in their relationships as consultancy styles are clarified. How intrusive does the consultant need to be during sessions? Does the consultant get 'sucked in' to becoming a third therapist? Does the consultant not intervene enough for fear of disqualification by the therapists?

Teams will face their own difficulties and experiment with solutions as consultant–therapist roles clarify and develop over time. The conflict is usually ultimately creative, and if the team remains aware of the significance of its own internal processes, it will develop the most effective possible model.

'Ad hoc' *teams*

Participation in *ad hoc* teams quickly became a regular part of the overall work of the staff members. Social workers from the social services department would join the NSPCC workers for a specific assessment. These would remain NSPCC teams, making recommendations to the appropriate local authority at the end of the work in the usual way. It is usually the social worker involved with a particular family and anxious for an opportunity to experience a different style of working who makes the request for an *ad hoc* team. The experience of considerable therapeutic freedom within a tight statutory structure is quite different from the usual work setting of most social workers.

We learned from painful experience to consider carefully how *viable* a proposed *ad hoc* team is likely to be. Once a request for an *ad hoc* team has been received, it is important to meet with the social services area manager to establish what it really represents. What are the hidden agendas? If these are not dealt with at this stage, the team will certainly trip over them later to the detriment of its work with the family. When such issues have been explored, a 'contract' will be agreed defining the status of the *ad hoc* team; as part of this the area manager will commit him or herself to releasing the two social services workers for all of the time required – and if necessary to cover their other duties for them.

Contract for NSPCC assessment team

1. The assessment will be by the NSPCC Child Protection Team.

2. All decisions re case management, therapy, and the eventual recommendation will be made by the NSPCC team during the period of the assessment.

3. The NSPCC team will consist of A [therapist] and B [consultant], joined by C [social services department worker] and D [senior social services department worker] who will become part of the NSPCC team.

4. Each member agrees to attend all sessions including de-briefings. E [social services department area manager] agrees to release and cover for C and D for all sessions.

5. Recording will be completed by the consultant.

6. The team will liaise with the foster home, and C will undertake the boarding-out visits.

Signed by A, B, C, D, E

It is important to examine the viability of *ad hoc* teams and to recognize that some proposed arrangements are unlikely to work. It is the responsibility of the staff members to test out such issues as carefully as seems necessary. Once the composition of an *ad hoc* team has been agreed, a couple of half-day 'team-building' exercises may follow, particularly if the members involved have not previously worked together.

Initial contact with the family

At the point when the statutory order has been made, or before if they are not contesting the order, the parents will be given an information leaflet describing the general conditions which will apply during the assessment:

'Welcome to working with the Rochdale NSPCC Child Protection Team. To complete an assessment with us depends on basic agreement between your family and the Team who have been asked to work with you. The Team have been asked to provide an assessment of your family and to make a recommendation about the future of your child(ren). The Team consists of . . . [names].

The seriousness of your situation demands that you are absolutely committed to the assessment work. Cooperation with the Team involves several basic requirements:

1. You must contact the Team if for any reason you cannot keep an appointment.

2. You must cooperate with the work requested.

3. From time to time tasks will be set, sometimes for completion between sessions. You will complete all set tasks.

4. All members of the family required for particular sessions will attend.

5. You agree not to use physical violence towards anyone in the sessions.

6. You will be asked to sign a further agreement relating to the Team's work with your particular family.

7. The assessment will take place using video recording equipment and a room with a one way mirror. These facilities are essential for us to provide you with the best possible service. Video tapes are confidential and will only be used for purposes outside of the assessment with your written permission.

In this agreement we have given you many responsibilities, some of which may be difficult for you. Nevertheless, we expect you to live up to them. We accept our responsibility to provide the best possible assessment of your family.'

The information leaflet provides some written information for parents to prepare them for their initial session with the team; the referring social worker will probably also have provided a great deal more information. Some parents discuss the information leaflet with their solicitors, and this is encouraged.

All assessment sessions take place on the child protection team's premises – known as 'The Unit'. The invitation for the initial appointment will be sent by letter, and this first session will be used to clarify the parents' understanding of what the assessment will entail.

Therapeutic control

In a way similar to that described by Sgroi (1982) in the field of sexual abuse, the team stresses the importance of therapeutic control with involuntary clients subject to statutory child-protection orders. Power is inescapably an issue for agencies and teams attempting to intervene therapeutically with child-abusing families. The usefulness – indeed the largely unrecognized therapeutic potential – of powerful statutory mandates to engage highly resistant families in assessment and therapy is demonstrated in this book. There has been a tendency for professional social workers to deny or minimize the reality of their statutory power over abusing families. Many individual workers feel much discomfort about exercising therapeutic authority, and allow themselves to be rapidly divested of it by families whose own power they choose not to recognize.

The trend towards therapeutic team work may be seen as a mechanism to strengthen the therapist against the increasingly recognized power of such families. Reference has been made in Chapter 1 to Hoffman's vivid description of the 'therapeutic contest' which takes place between families and (strategic) family therapy teams (Hoffman 1981: 328–29). Sgroi, pressing the need for a firm and overt use of therapeutic authority with sexually abusing families, comments: 'No matter how attractive, competent, and optimistic we appear, these clients will turn to us only as an alternative to some pressure or sanction' (Sgroi 1982: 3).

The Rochdale team's assessment work with involuntary clients centres on the structured use of control in a therapeutic setting. The most obvious manifestations of this orientation are the following:

'Clinical setting'

All assessment work takes place in sessions held at the Unit and these are by appointment and time-limited, usually to an hour and a half. Earlier experience of other settings, for example family therapy in clients' homes, confirmed the therapeutic value of using our own territory for seeing families. Contact with families between sessions is discouraged (apart from real emergencies) and parents recognize that little help will be forthcoming in practical family matters. This may contrast sharply with high levels of practical assistance given perhaps by previous social workers and other professionals. Overall, surprisingly few of the families we see following serious child abuse have significant financial or material problems.

Families are introduced to a *team* of three or four workers, whose various roles are briefly explained to them. The paraphernalia of the interviewing room is demonstrated – the one-way screen, camera, and microphones; and most families accept the invitation to visit 'behind the screen' to see how the room looks from the other side. The purpose of these facilities is explained in a low-key way, and there is seldom any objection from parents to their being used.

If objections become a significant problem, then this will provide the *content* focus for the team's exploration of the parents' processes of resistance. In our experience, sexually abusing families are initially more sensitive to the use of the one-way mirror and video than families in which physical abuse has occurred. Objecting to working in a room with a one-way mirror invariably provides the most obvious 'hook' on which parents can hang their resistance to the assessment and to their resented status as involuntary clients.

It is essential to deal with the *process* of the resistance as such, and not to get involved in *content* arguments or negotiations, for example about using a different room. Such objections can almost invariably be overcome in the initial session, if the team focuses on their process and wider meaning. The team must remember, however, that ultimately parents should retain the right *not* to be filmed if their objection remains firm. But the team will not concede to a parental refusal to the use of the one-way mirror, as this is seen as crucial to the effectiveness of our work.

In reality, the use of these technical facilities rarely becomes an issue, the parents' reactions more typically being indifference, inquisitiveness, or even amusement. Families very quickly adjust to the setting, usually far more easily than the outside social workers in an '*ad hoc*' team.

Clearing the ring

Apart from these factors, there are important changes in other relationships which serve to reinforce the structure of the overall therapeutic model. Of particular importance would be the intervention by the team in the inter-agency system to obtain specific clarification of the role of each significant other agency during the period of contact with the family. It is usual for the team to press for a general 'clearing of the ring', that is for the other agencies to withdraw or significantly limit their involvements during this time. Usually this is agreed to with relief. Such a clarification of roles is vitally important as it lessens the family's scope for manipulative behaviour towards different professionals, and also gives the first hint to the agencies and the family alike that a process is beginning whereby the family is taking back responsibility for itself.

Contracts

Contracts in a social work and therapeutic context are written agreements between the participants to clarify the rules and expectations of a relationship. They have no legal status, although they may become significant in subsequent legal proceedings in cases where parents choose not to comply with the requirements of the assessment. For each assessment an individual contract will be drawn up by the team relating to its proposed work with that particular family. Contracts are used to specify the team's requirements of the family during the period of assessment, and also to detail the service which will be provided. They define the team's conditions for work with the family, are carefully prepared, and contain simple and unnegotiable statements.

Typically, a contract will specify points such as: sessions must begin and end on time; the family must co-operate with work focusing on their current and past difficulties and relationships; the attendance of extended-family members or other significant people at sessions may be requested; the permitted access of parents to children in care is stated, and it is required that the parents behave reasonably during such contact.

It is important to anticipate and include within the contract the issues which are likely to be contentious or of particular significance. This allows the team to elicit much of the family's resistance at an early stage rather than to encounter it unexpectedly later on. The usefulness of this technique may be illustrated by the example of a family in which both parents were addicted to heroin, and the local authority had obtained a parental rights resolution on their child on the grounds of 'mode of life'. At an initial clarification meeting the mother insisted that she was quite prepared to participate in all of the work described, except that she was not prepared to talk about the death of her first child in an accident some ten years earlier. The team insisted that it would require agreement that every event of significance in the family history should be open for discussion. With some protest both parents eventually agreed. Several weeks later when this historical material was reached, the mother became intensely emotionally involved in talking about the lost child and her continuing feelings of guilt for the circumstances of the accident. She later acknowledged that since the child had died she had never spoken openly to anyone about the incident or her guilty feelings.

The imaginative use of contracts tailored to each specific family situation can even include optional clauses enabling parents to begin working towards decisions on areas which will be crucial during the forthcoming assessment work. An example of this occurred with the same parents whose continued use of heroin was a significant issue. Part of their contract contained the following two options, of which they had to select one:

'8.1 During the course of the assessment neither parent uses heroin or any other drug illegally. No illegal drugs are allowed into the home, and no drug users are allowed into the home.
8.2 During the course of the assessment, whilst [the child] is visiting the home, no illegal drugs or drug users will be allowed into the home. As parents, if use of heroin continues to be an issue, you agree to be open about this in sessions, and if necessary to seek appropriate medical/psychiatric treatment.'

The parents thought hard about which of these two conditions was the most realistic for them. They decided together between sessions that they would go for the tougher option of 8.1. They came to the next session with the whole contract signed, and 8.2 crossed out. A contract with optional choices fitted the task the couple had set *themselves* during the assessment – to stay off drugs completely. As part of this, they agreed willingly to an additional clause stating that they would co-operate with unannounced urine testing by their doctor when requested by the team. At one point a urine test *was* found to have a positive trace of opiates. It became clear that this was not due to heroin but to a proprietary pain killer containing codeine prescribed for influenza. The parents then agreed to take no more codeine during the assessment.

Structure of sessions

Assessment sessions tend to fall into a structure of five stages, and this organization of work is an important means of maintaining maximum energy and impetus.

Pre-briefing

Pre-briefing involves discussion between the therapeutic team to plan the content and aims of the session. A general principle is that all sessions have specific aims and purposes, the achievement of which can be assessed subsequently at the de-briefing stage. A focus for each session will usually be worked out at the pre-briefing, and this will reflect the particular stage the assessment has reached. Nevertheless, the team will always maintain an awareness of 'here and now' processes within the room, whether these be to do with issues between the parents, or between the parents and the therapists.

Therapeutic power and effectiveness often stem from the identification of significant issues through a process-based exploration of matters which superficially may appear minor or even trivial. Such interventions and the positive changes which result are of more significance than the gathering of information which is also a central part of the assessment work. This information provides essential material about the pathology and dangerousness in the family history; process interventions provide the means of exploring the family's ability to change.

Ad hoc teams frequently find that the outside workers need to work hard to adjust to such heavily process-based interventions, which seem to them unfamiliar and uncomfortable; they are also encouraged to examine their more habitual responses which are often based on 'rescuing' or conflict avoidance. The team will of course need to explore these reactions within its own processes, and for the inexperienced workers this provides a useful practice base from which to explore associated processes within the family, and between the family and the therapists.

The session

Armed with an agreed plan for the session, together with a readiness to change direction and focus on an observed 'here and now' issue, the therapists will join the family. The content and emotional tone of the session will reflect the current level of resistance, and the stage the information-seeking activity has reached. The mood will range from tension and anger (either between the parents, or between them and the therapists) to emotionally cathartic re-experiencing of painful events. In other situations the emotional tone may be inappropriately flat, the therapists becoming subject to bouts of boredom with parents who are passive and unexpressive.

One of the functions of the consultant is to make sure that the therapists remain in control of the session, but that is not to say that they necessarily adopt a controlling stance *within* the session. A useful rule of thumb for the consultant is to intervene when the therapists seem to be doing 'more than 50 per cent' of the work. The consultant will try to help the therapists who may be getting 'stuck' in unproductive or repetitive transactions. Working too hard with passive families or arguing with angry families are common examples.

Passive families lure therapists into bombarding them with questions in the hope of hitting on something that they will answer, so at least some form of dialogue – or something – can be seen to be happening. As will be described later in this chapter, passivity is a very powerful and controlling form of resistance. What is needed is a response which begins to explore the *process* of passivity for that particular family – what it helps them gain and what it helps them avoid. As part of such a response it will often be useful for the therapists to begin to *mirror* the family's own passivity – so that instead of constant activity through questioning, silences will be employed.

On the other hand sessions at the stage when the parents are thoroughly engaged in the process of work will have an active and businesslike atmosphere as the parents work on the sorts of tasks and activities which will be described in the next chapter.

Breaks

Breaks are taken during sessions for a variety of reasons; during such times the family are left alone, unobserved and unrecorded. Breaks may occur to create some space to consider an issue within the therapeutic system (the relationship between the therapists and the family), or because of a matter which has arisen within the team itself. In the former case, the therapists may wish to interrupt or recover from a stormy, violent blast from a hostile family, and to review or consolidate the strategy being employed to deal with this hostility.

On the other hand a break may be taken when the therapists are conscious that they have become totally bored and uninspired with a family in which passivity and hopelessness predominate. The team will need to work to re-energize itself – but not in a way which involves starting to do the work of the family for them. Breaks are particularly useful during periods of resistance, and at such times the family may be left alone to struggle with an important decision. In that context breaks can be used to create an intensification of the emotional effect which in itself is often a very potent therapeutic tool.

Breaks will also be necessary to deal with difficult issues which arise within the team. There may be a lack of congruence between the therapists, or between the therapists and the consultant. When such issues arise – as they will in all teams working creatively – it is important that they be *explored*, rather than avoided and some quick compromise found. The creativity and energy of the team will stem from the operation and exploration of its members' differences rather than from their similarities. A common question therefore during a break is which of several appropriate and available therapeutic paths to follow. The consultant may observe that the two therapists have different inclinations as to how to proceed, and may feel that both options are likely to be productive. The consultant may stay 'meta' to the therapists' disagreement (for example giving them a time-limit within which to find an agreed way to proceed), or he or she may become drawn into taking sides or even coming up with a different proposal.

Such disagreements tend to be resolved in different ways for staff teams than for *ad hoc* teams. For *ad hoc* teams, if an open examination of the processes lying behind the disagreement is not sufficient to resolve it (as it usually is), then the clause in the team contract giving the staff member the final say must be invoked. This is an important clause for the staff team, as their primary responsibility is for the effectiveness of the work with the family.

Return

Important issues will have been discussed by the team during the break and often this will result in the therapists changing focus or style on the resumption of the session. If the break was called as a way of dealing with an issue of 'stuckness' between the therapists and the parents, then either the issue in question will remain under focus or a statement will be made that the work appears to have reached an impasse. There will be a firm implication that it is the task of the parents to find a way to resolve this.

If the break occurred because of a difference within the team, over alternative ways of proceeding for example, it may be useful to inform the family what the disagreement was about. The pros and cons of the options discussed may be outlined to the family, and an element of humour may be introduced as the team caricatures its own 'squabbling' processes to the family. This is especially powerful when the difference in the team is felt to mirror a difference in the family, or to have been 'set up' or provoked by the parents.

Alternatively, the parents may be given no information about the content of the break, but will clearly experience a difference in the therapists on their return. Work may even continue exactly where it left off. Often, breaks are called just before the end of a session, and the team may have used the time to decide what homework to set the family between sessions.

De-briefing

De-briefing meetings follow immediately after the session with the family, and are used partially to review the session in terms of the goals established beforehand, and the significant events and developments. De-briefing also enables the team to wind down after the intellectual and emotional exertion which such work often entails. Observers would be bemused and not a little offended by the team's comments and general behaviour at such moments. Black humour is a predominant feature, and serves the essential purpose of allowing anxiety, anger, and a range of other emotions to be discharged. Guitars and many therapeutic toys are usually to hand, and de-briefings following dramatic or particularly significant sessions often turn into maniacal jam-sessions! Unfortunately these usually seem to happen at the precise moment that senior management or important visitors are arriving!

A different mood may be created when work with a family has caused stress within the therapeutic team and this needs to be faced further in de-briefing. It is essential that the whole team take responsibility for looking at the underlying issues. It is interesting to note that in the course of development of our team, as the dominant therapeutic principles have evolved away from the original focus on strategic family therapy and towards the more experiential-type therapies (particularly *Gestalt*), the issues within the team have changed accordingly. Our use of the strategic family therapy model was mirrored in a period of power struggles within the team, and a good deal of covert activity and communication. The *Gestalt* influence has been mirrored in a detailed and at times painful examination of team processes and relationships, and has been characterized by progression to much more open, creative communication.

The five stages described for a session with a family, though not rigidly adhered to, provide a useful structure for the organization of work. Similarly, all of the factors described in this section under 'therapeutic control' provide an important element of consistency for the family during the assessment. A secure and predictable environment is provided: this is of basic significance to many families, particularly those which have been characterized as being 'out of control' – both in respect of their internal relationships and their relationships with outside agencies. It is likely that the provision of the statutory therapeutic context, together with the response made to deal with the parents' initial resistance to it, is as important for subsequent change as the more direct therapeutic work which occurs later.

Resistance

It has already been observed that families respond to the imposition of therapeutic control with overt or covert forms of resistance. Resistance, however, is an ally of the therapist, as Freud for one was well aware:

> 'In the first place, when we undertake to restore a patient to health, to relieve him of the symptoms of his illness, he meets us with a violent and tenacious resistance which persists through-out the whole length of the treatment . . . the patient's resistance is often of very many sorts, extremely subtle and often hard to detect. . . . Resistances . . . should not be one-sidedly condemned. They include so much of the most important material from the patient's past and bring it back in so convincing a fashion that they become some of the best supports of an analysis if a skilled technique knows how to give them the right turn.'
> (Freud 1916: 332)

Freud's explanation of this phenomenon of resistance to the removal of symptoms was: 'We tell ourselves that we have succeeded in discovering powerful forces which oppose any alteration of the patient's condition; they must be the same ones which in the past brought that condition about' (Freud 1916: 334).

Phenomena of resistance can also be seen as a feature of the systemic behaviour of families. The tendency of family systems to resist change and stick with established patterns of behaviour has been described in Chapter 1. Family systems often become 'stuck' in unsatisfying (and, in the case of child abuse, dangerous) sets of relationships which nevertheless provide the most comfortable roles for the members to exist within. It is important for therapists to recognize that these powerful processes exist within family systems to sustain distorted transactions, no matter how apparently discomforting or unsatisfying to members they may be. The resistance involved in maintaining equilibrium in the family system is a feature of all family processes, and therapy attempts to channel this positively.

Resistance, however, is not something that families 'have', and 'bring' with them to sessions; the resistance is a relationship with, and a response to, their initial encounter with the team. It has a communication function. It is a response to the prospect of change.

The meeting of the parents and the team in the circumstances described triggers the formation of a new system – the 'therapeutic' system which will need to develop its own internal rules and patterns of behaviour. The dynamics of this system will be crucial throughout the assessment. Issues of power and control will be tested out between the parties, and often a 'therapeutic contest' will ensue. The resistance manifested by the parents to the non-negotiable terms of the assessment, together with their position as involuntary clients, makes it crucially important that the authority of the team should be maintained at this stage.

Types of resistance

It is possible to characterize three general types of resistance encountered by the therapists at the initial stage of an assessment with a family. The response of the parents usually fits into one of the following descriptions.

Hostile

Hostile resistance is characterized by overt anger on the part of the parents, which may include a range of physical and legal threats. In first interviews there will be a determined challenge to the team's authority and competence. There will be evidence of an overt lack of trust, general suspiciousness, and denial of responsibility for the injury or other circumstances that led to the child coming into care. Such families often have long histories of battles with a large number of social agencies.

Passive–aggressive

Passive–aggressive resistance is characterized by *covert* anger which conceals a powerful underlying denial and avoidance. There is a covert lack of trust beneath an initial presentation which is likely to be polite, if not obsequious. Such parents may present as being highly critical of the way they have been treated by other agencies, and may be flattering towards the team and deferential to the 'experts'. However, it quickly becomes apparent that such co-operation and recognition of concern are only *superficial*, masking a process of withholding significant information and feelings; and levels of deviousness and rationalization between the couple based on an enmeshed and highly collusive relationship.

Passive–hopeless

Passive–hopeless resistance is manifested by personalities and relationships which appear to be 'caving in' and disintegrating, and where the parents' own energy levels and commitment seem insufficient to maintain themselves, let alone to work towards the reconstitution of the family. The parents' attitudes and presentation to the therapists may be characterized by degrees of depression, despair, and guilt. Usually there is a total but overwhelming acknowledgement of problems, with the implication that no change is possible, or that the team must provide a solution. Parents look for a dependent relationship, and may have a history of attracting and defeating previous helpers with a 'rescuing' stance.

Engagement strategies

Engagement strategies are simple therapeutic techniques which are employed to counter a family's resistance to the assessment context and to promote their energetic commitment to the therapeutic opportunity which is offered. The following three general principles lie behind all engagement strategies.

Neutral attitude of the therapists

Responsibility for whether or not to accept the work on offer is the parents'. The therapists will offer clarification, but will not intervene to 'help' the parents to come to a decision. Often the parents' struggle with this decision is an intensification of their efforts to solve many of the significant problems they have experienced in the outside world. The therapists will reflect openly on such possibilities, but will always stress that it is the parents' choice at that moment whether or not to participate in the work on offer.

Focus on process rather than content

The importance of this as a fundamental therapeutic principle cannot be overemphasized. The difference between process and content issues was outlined in Chapter 1 (p. 12). When two parents are struggling with a decision about whether or not to sign the contract, the therapists may direct their attention to the process of how important decisions are taken in their relationship. In many cases such moments provide significant direct information about the dynamics of that spouse relationship; consequently the assessment has already begun.

Promotion of a change of emotional affect

Usually, parents manifest one particular emotional tone predominantly at initial sessions. This may be anger, sadness, despair, passivity, or even an inappropriate levity. The mood may seem to be firmly 'stuck', and at such times it can be therapeutically potent to use some simple techniques to test out how changeable such moods are. Often the therapist may experience such predominant emotions as being somewhat transparent or inauthentic, and when this is so, it can be very productive to explore intuitively the emotion that seems to be missing.

A simple technique is for the therapist to think of the best single adjective to describe the parents' mood, and then to explore issues around the *opposite*, or an associated, emotion. When the mood is depressed it is invariably fruitful to explore how *anger* in the family and the individual personalities is inhibited. Similarly feelings of fear, hurt, and rejection can be explored to great effect in people who present as being really angry with others. In such situations the therapists may comment on the use of depression and anger as masks or shields against feelings of wanting to attack or of being attacked.

This technique is often effective in dealing with anger, which characterizes the hostile type of resistance, and suspiciousness, which is typical of the passive–aggressive response. It is particularly useful when such emotions come predominantly from one partner and are not actively reinforced by the other. Instead, the spouse may be upset and demonstrate a vulnerable sensitivity which is also likely to be present in the more openly hostile partner. The principle also applies in reverse – the 'upset' partner is also likely to be containing equivalent angry feelings.

By using such techniques which disregard the parents' emotional masks, a rapid and genuine emotional contact can be made with the more authentic feelings which lie behind. This provides a major step towards engagement, and the establishment of a therapeutic rapport.

In the initial manifestation of resistance at the beginning of an assessment, it is the hostile families who present the most anxiety-provoking and spectacular incidents. Such parents often arrive well aware of their fearful reputations! It was observed in Chapter 2 that the people who frighten professionals the most are not necessarily the most dangerous. Threats and violence in habitually threatening and violent personalities are used with a good deal of measured control. In our experience of hostile families at the initial stage, some of the techniques described offer considerable potential for overcoming resistance and creating a therapeutic engagement. The process of tackling hostile resistance at the initial stage is consistent enough to allow the presentation of a typical pattern:

Family behaviour	*Therapists' behaviour*
1. The parents arrive for their session and *argue* about the context, e.g. they denounce the unjustness of the care order, deny responsibility for the injury, produce counter-allegations, etc. Parents insist that they have been put in their present position by some mistake, and disqualify the role and competence of the team.	Therapists refuse to become involved in these well-rehearsed arguments. There is no response to the content. Instead, process questions are asked about what is happening in the room, e.g. Is it always father who argues? The quieter partner may be asked how long the other will argue for, and what will happen next? Will she take over? Is he going to hit me? How will the argument end?
	After time spent learning about the processes of the couple's anger, a positive connotation of their feelings may be used; this may be a

Family behaviour	*Therapists' behaviour*
	statement by the therapists recognizing that the anger is a clear statement of the parents' concern for, and commitment to, their child.
2. The parents stop arguing.	Continuing to deal with the 'here and now' processes the couple may be asked: How long can they sit without arguing? How will they start arguing again? Who will start? Further anger is thus anticipated and predicted. (This involves the use of paradox – the therapists begin to assume some control over the anger. The effectiveness of the anger is also diminished as the therapists show some appreciation of it. Parents find it difficult to maintain hostile responses to statements that their behaviour shows concern for the child – which is usually, but not always, true.)
3. The parents begin arguing again.	Therapists may gently – and carefully – introduce an element of *humour*. This may be done by attaching humorous labels to the process of the anger. The therapists may enquire about family metaphors for such anger which undoubtedly also occurs in the family setting. What do the parents call their angry

Family behaviour   *Therapists' behaviour*

outbursts? What do the
extended family call it? The
process of *threat* within the
room can also be addressed:
How frightened should we be of
you? How will we know when
we are not safe?

*Humorous labelling of an
identified angry process
devalues it in a way which is not
unrewarding for the family.*
Humour often also provides a
'stand-down' position for
people who are angry enabling
them to avoid feeling that they
are losing face or have been
beaten in a battle. Clearly such
techniques must be used with
care, and with reference to the
actual physical risk which the
therapists experience. Humour
is indicated more often in an
atmosphere of projected anger,
than in the much rarer
encounters of menace.

4. The parents become
confused.

Therapists comment on the
process of the confusion –
asking 'information' questions:
What's happening? What will
happen next? This may be the
point to explore a significant
associated emotion. Otherwise
there may be a clear statement
of the family's predicament and
options. The parents are told
they must make a decision as to
whether they are going to

Family behaviour	*Therapists' behaviour*
	continue being 'stroppy' (or their metaphor), or sign the contract and begin work.
5. Parents begin arguing again, *but* now about the *content* of the contract.	Therapists reassert that the contract is non-negotiable, and restate the parents' responsibility to take a decision. Some form of time-limit may be set. Therapists may explore the couple's decision-making processes further: how will they decide whether to sign or not? *Who* will decide? Will the other partner sabotage this? Will they continue arguing with each other so as not to take a decision?
6. (a) The parents agree to sign and do so.	Signing by the team. Practical arrangements worked out about next session and future appointments.
(b) Parents continue arguing about the content of the contract.	Therapists state that the parents are unable to decide, and prefer to continue arguing. Parents must take a decision for themselves and inform the team.
End of session	*End of session*
	A follow-up letter may be sent immediately after the session reinforcing the tension; it will restate the parents' dilemmas

Family behaviour   *Therapists' behaviour*

and options, and comment that the team does not know what their decision will be. An appointment for the next session will be included. It is up to the family to cancel if they want to.

7. The parents arrive for the second session.

Therapists explore the process of how they decided to come. Who decided? Who opposed? Who agreed? Who most wanted to come? Was there an argument or a fight about taking the decision? Was the extended family an influence? Therapists state the need for the contract to be signed, or there is no point in continuing the session.

8. Parents sign.

Walk-outs

Occasionally this process may be interrupted at some point by a 'walk-out' by either or both parents. Walk-outs are often significant moments, and not uncommonly can be identified retrospectively as the beginning of positive change. Walk-outs involve the parents in actively taking a decision, and the processes involved in this provide important information as to how the family functions. Does one partner only walk out, or do they both leave simultaneously? Does one partner show hesitation or reluctance?

Walk-outs leave the parents both separately and together with an acute dilemma – are they to return? The week at home before the next appointment is a turning-point in the relationship of many couples. It is not uncommon for separations to occur at this point, perhaps with a stepparent leaving. In such circumstances the natural parent may engage in the assessment actively as a single parent. Most couples, however, do return as couples to accept the contract, and this is often a significant step on their part.

The engagement phase of work with child-abusing families is demanding but crucial for the outcome of the assessment. The understanding gained about the way the family operates as it encounters the team will provide significant pointers for the therapists to identify important processes which should be focused on throughout the assessment. Such sessions also provide a base-line against which to measure changes in attitudes, behaviour, and relationships which may occur as work progresses.

CHAPTER 5

Assessment

After the stage of countering the initial resistance of the parents, work in assessments tends to follow a defined but flexible pattern. A contract defining the context of the assessment will have been signed, and the team and the family will be anticipating weekly sessions for a period of between three and four months until a recommendation about the future of the children is made.

Genograms

After the initial, often tense, first sessions, the focus is likely to shift away from the 'here and now' on to the compilation and exploration of each parent's genogram, or family tree. The process of working on genograms takes attention away from contentious recent issues, and promotes a less tense environment for 'joining' between the therapists and the parents to occur.

Through the compilation of large family trees covering the previous two or three generations, a great deal of information about significant family events and relationships is obtained. In addition to providing knowledge about relevant stress factors, a picture emerges of the operation of the family systems over several generations. Genograms allow for a comprehensive and systematic collection of history, and build up a store of information about the 'journey through life so far' of the parents who have come to abuse their own child.

This stage of work also allows the therapists to identify issues within the histories described which represent the parents' 'unfinished business' from previous relationships; often a highly effective therapeutic intervention can be made at this time. It is often productive to use non-verbal techniques to represent relationships: for example, plastic 'play people' can be used to portray interactions; and drawings, particularly cartoons of significant family members, can provide a substantial basis for therapeutic exploration. Many social workers are skilled at using drawing and symbols in work with children – the same techniques are equally potent with their parents.

The compilation of genograms often leads to the identification of unresolved emotional issues which require a therapeutic response. Most striking in our experience is the significant proportion of physically abusing mothers who report that they were sexually abused in their childhood and have never had the opportunity to work through this in a therapeutic setting, in fact often have never mentioned it before. The team will need to be clear as to whether the therapeutic work will be undertaken at this stage, or whether the issues need to be acknowledged and the work postponed until a later stage. The need to make a decision about the children will be the prime consideration.

Current behaviour in individuals and families, which appears to make little sense when viewed from a 'here and now' perspective, can be understood surprisingly well when viewed as 'unfinished business' from previous experiences. The position of grandparents on both sides is often very significant, and working through genograms makes it possible to understand their continuing role in the present-day life of the family.

Often the role of grandparents and other extended family members is one of involvement, but not of a consistently helpful kind. Such involvement may be extremely destructive and undermining of the parents' abilities and confidence. Alternatively, extended family members who appear to be in a position to offer support may not be doing so, and it is useful to explore the reasons for this. In many cases it will be to do with historical conflicts in the family, conflicts which may have been connected with the parents' leaving home in the first place and having children at an early age. In such situations it is appropriate to invite the important extended family members to a session early on in the assessment; this can result in significant progress in resolving such historical disputes which are often thoroughly 'stuck'. If no such progress occurs, there will be in any event a useful open clarification about the potential – or lack of it – for support within the extended family system. Following such sessions it is not unusual for parents to develop an understanding of their need to detach themselves from other family members (usually their parents) with whom they have previously been in a dependent relationship.

During work on the genograms, observations will be made as to the spouse relationship, and how this functions around issues of openness, adaptability, power, and recognition of, and responsiveness to, each other's needs. Such observations provide the base-line from which to view changes which are likely to occur during the assessment.

The process of this work may also generate a change of atmosphere within the therapeutic system. This may be reflected in changes in the way information is given. Do the therapists have to work hard, constantly asking questions which produce only specific, limited replies? Or do the parents quickly become emotionally involved in the exercise, working spontaneously and anecdotally? What is the emotional affect and presentation when significant areas are reached? What is the response to a therapeutic focus on feelings at such times? Do the parents block such moves, or do they wish to make use of the therapeutic opportunities presented to cry, to feel guilty, or to be angry?

Before an assessment begins, the team will have obtained a good deal of information from the records of other agencies about the significant events and history relating to that particular family. It will be very important to consider how the parents' account of these matters fits with the agency versions. What is the level of information presented? How does this match other recorded accounts? When there are discrepancies it is important that the therapists explore these carefully. It may be necessary to check the accuracy of the written agency records by interviewing previous professionals involved with the family.

When there are significant discrepancies between agency records of previous events (perhaps an earlier injury) and the parents' account of them, and the records can be proved accurate, then the onus in the sessions will be on the parents to explain the difference. At such times, parental resistance is likely to recur forcefully.

An example of this is two parents who had served prison sentences following a verdict of manslaughter on their two-year-old daughter. The mother was five months pregnant, and the team were working on an assessment of whether they could be allowed to care for the baby. Both parents stated that they had only mildly chastised the child in the two weeks before her death, and that they found it difficult to understand how she had come to die. They did acknowledge that they had had sole care of her.

The pathologist's report was five pages long, and documented eighty different injuries, including five fractured ribs and multiple bruising, all dated to within seven days of the child's death. Despite sustained efforts by the team, the parents refused to move from their position of extreme *minimization* of what they had been responsible for. The baby was taken into care at birth and subsequently adopted.

Resistance may take other forms when a significant area for the parents is reached in an assessment. It may be unexpected and take the therapists by surprise. It is vital that at such moments the therapists focus on the process of what is happening. The content may seem trivial but the team will need to work towards an understanding of how it connects with something very important.

In one assessment case the team was struggling with a single mother who consistently maintained a passive–aggressive resistance and refused to allow any access to the real feelings beneath her punctual attendance and superficial co-operation. Nothing the therapist did had any effect until he was accidently twenty minutes late for a session. The mother was absolutely furious and harangued him very aggressively for almost half an hour before dissolving into bitter tears. During this period the therapist said nothing, realizing that something very important was happening for this mother which he had inadvertently sparked off, but otherwise had no real part in. He was the 'here and now' representative of whatever unfinished business with others the mother was working on; and being aware of this, *he was quite prepared to play the part.* More progress was made in that single session than the previous six.

Genogram sessions often reveal disastrous individual and family biographies including histories of physical and sexual abuse; damaging upbringings in 'care'; experiences of numerous step-parents; and chronic emotional deprivation leading to 'failure to exist' scripts which develop into 'failure to protect' or violent parenting roles.

Some parents suspect that the whole assessment process is simply geared towards obtaining extra evidence for keeping their children in care, or removing those still at home. It is important when such attitudes appear to be 'in the air' that the therapists recognize them openly and comment on them, so that the process can become an overt issue. Invariably such suspicions will reflect the parents' generalized lack of trust in the world, which at that moment the therapists represent. At such times it is crucial for the therapists not to offer inappropriate reassurances, as this is not helpful to parents who are struggling with fundamental issues of basic trust. Instead, the therapists might comment on the parents' dilemma as to whether they can trust them and might suggest that they take great care in reaching their conclusion.

Spouse relationship

Once the individual genograms reach the point where the parents first met, the history of the couple's relationship will be considered. By this point it is likely that the experience of the assessment so far has had some effect on their relationship. It may be that the level of tension in an already unstable relationship has increased; if so, the therapists will have already focused on this. Occasionally couples separate in the early stage of an assessment, most commonly by the stepfather leaving the family. This is always a manifestation that the unviability of a relationship has become overt. When this happens, it often 'frees' the remaining partner from a defensive collusion and leads to his or her more genuine engagement in the assessment as a single parent.

In other cases, the sharing of the detailed biographical material raises issues which most couples begin to work on themselves, either within or outside sessions. Events and relationships may be revealed that the other partner did not know about; or previously concealed attitudes and emotional experiences may emerge. From the beginning the therapists openly assume that they have permission to explore all issues within the family histories, and that if there are significant gaps in one partner's knowledge about the other which are likely to be revealed in sessions, then the couple themselves will rectify this between sessions.

This initial statement provides the context for openness and sharing between the partners; if the possibility of significant secrets has been an issue, these have usually been shared before they are reached in the genogram session. In many cases the genogram work leads to a consolidation of the parents' relationship.

The history gathering will continue to cover the parents' relationship. How did the couple meet? What were the attitudes of other family members to their relationship? How long has the relationship lasted? How does this compare with their previous relationships? Have there been separations and reconciliations? If so, these will be considered in detail to establish the specific pattern of satisfactions and dissatisfactions in the relationship.

Other couples will present as being highly collusive and will deny any disagreements or tension within their relationship. Such couples relate to the therapists in a passive–aggressive way; invariably, they also *relate to each other* in a passive–aggressive way. They manifest a relationship of *denied dissatisfaction* which contains an element of explosive violence. In such couples, each partner often looks to the children for the satisfaction of his or her emotional needs, in an atmosphere of unspoken disappointment and frustration that the other partner no longer meets these needs. The *child* is then scapegoated and abused for the lack of parental satisfaction and for making his or her own demands. Both parents may abuse the child, or one may adopt a failure-to-protect role. The parents collude to project the internal threat to their relationship (the denied dissatisfactions) on to a third party. A child who becomes the object of such projections is at very serious risk. The assessment will focus throughout on the dynamics of the spouse relationship.

Genograms of the injured child and siblings

Although the children in the family will have appeared on the original genograms, it is often productive to reserve a specific session to take their histories in detail. To focus on the injured child marks a renewed focus on currently emotive and sensitive issues. Some form of resistance will inevitably recur or occur at this time, and the therapists will carefully explore its process. The area of greatest sensitivity may thus become quickly apparent, whether it is to do with parents denying responsibility, minimizing the events, or concealing an incriminating secret.

As the genograms of the children are compiled, the parents' attitudes regarding responsibility for past events – which may include histories of unsatisfactory care and previous injuries – will become clear. Responses will range from acceptance of guilt regarding such histories, to denial, minimization, or rationalization, with the blame placed elsewhere. Alternatively, parents may accept that their past behaviour gave cause for concern, but may still dissociate themselves from responsibility for it on the grounds that they have somehow changed since then.

Overall, the work on these genograms will produce a clear statement of the children's developmental and parenting history. Information from the records of other agencies, which is available through the case-conference system, will be vital in establishing a picture of parental strengths and weaknesses. If significant concern was felt about the child before the injury which led to the care order, it will be important to establish the exact reasons for this, and to review them with the parents. Was appropriate help offered by the agencies at that time? If so, did the parents use it appropriately? If not, why not? How do the parents feel about that now? Do they show signs of gaining sufficient maturity to view their past actions critically and to begin to accept that the concern was justified?

Injuries

The team will be aware throughout the assessment of whether the injury to the child was satisfactorily explained at the time of the initial investigations. In fatal and serious cases, despite police investigation, it is sometimes not possible to establish exactly what happened to the child. In such cases the parents or a parent may consistently admit to causing the injury, and consequently be convicted and sentenced in the criminal court. The acts of violence will be sufficient for the conviction; but the circumstances and relationships surrounding the abuse may not be revealed.

In rarer situations there may be intense collusion between the parents to conceal the causes of an injury and to maintain a consistent cover-up story. A five-year-old boy was admitted to hospital with a dislocated hip. Examinations revealed no congenital abnormality, and the consultant paediatrician described it as the most violent non-fatal injury he had ever seen. Throughout extensive police inquiries both parents remained resolute in their insistence that the injury had occurred when the boy fell over playing football. Expert medical opinion was equally resolute that this was impossible. It was not possible to charge either parent with any offence – there was no confession to any form of assault and no corroborative evidence of assault. After prolonged hospital treatment the boy was made subject to a care order on the grounds that he had been ill-treated. In this case there were other grounds for concern as well – including the fact that the five-year-old had insufficient speech to be able to explain what had happened to him.

In other situations, after a child has died or been seriously injured the parents may make allegations and counter-allegations against each other. One may make a statement which falsely implicates the other in causing the injury, or a person may falsely implicate himself or herself to protect the actual culprit.

It is not uncommon in assessments for parents who pleaded guilty to serious assaults on their child to claim that they did so because they were under pressure (either from the police or their solicitor), or because they feared that they would face a heavier sentence if they were found guilty after pleading not guilty.

The level of parental acceptance of responsibility for the injury (as opposed to continued denial or minimization) will be a crucial factor in determining the outcome of the assessment. In an assessment following fatal or serious child abuse the team will wish to be satisfied that the true story of the incident of abuse – and the role of each family member in it – has been established. Much effort will be put into sessions at this point to promote parental acceptance of responsibility and to challenge their process of minimization. The activity of the team will be geared towards testing out to what extent *change* is possible. They will have to give very careful thought to the behaviour of parents who refuse to provide missing information even when it has been made quite clear to them that this will have serious consequences for their unborn baby. It may be that the parents are communicating that there are greater, inviolable secrets to keep.

Some assessments will end when the parents are found to

remain unwilling to accept a realistic level of responsibility for the death or injury of the child. This invariably means that little has changed in their relationship, except that the collusion and enmeshment may have deepened.

In contrast, other parents may openly acknowledge the true circumstances of the injury and may express appropriate feelings of horror and remorse. They may thereby demonstrate that there have been significant changes in their lives and relationships since that time. The team will wish to focus on these changes: what exactly are they? who else has noticed? how did they occur?

Extended families

It is important to consider the reactions of the extended family to these events. What was the place of the deceased or injured child within the network of relatives? To what extent were other family members involved in taking care of the child and in the circumstances of the assaults? What are their levels of knowledge, understanding, and interpretation of what happened? To what extent are the parents now accepted or rejected within the extended family? How do the extended-family members feel about the process of the assessment and the decisions which may be reached?

Our experience has taught us to be constantly aware of the continuing power and pressure exerted on parents during assessments by their families of origin. When such issues seem to be influencing the process of work, it is always productive to invite the relevant extended-family members to a session to deal with them explicitly. We have worked with several families following serious child abuse where it became clear that the parents were under significant pressures from extended-family members *not* to acknowledge responsibility for the injuries. It may be that previously the extended family had firmly supported the parents in their original denial that they had been responsible. This support may have been based on an emotive belief that the parents could not have been responsible, or it may have been arranged as part of a collusive cover-up. In either situation it is difficult for a parent to face the repercussions in the extended family which are likely to follow from an open acceptance of responsibility at such a late stage.

In one assessment following an extremely serious case of prolonged abuse, the mother was ultimately able to acknowledge the reality of her involvement in the events, and to get in touch with her own horror at her behaviour. She had previously always adamantly denied being responsible and had been supported in this denial by her invalid mother.

The mother developed a real fear that her own mother would suffer another heart attack as a result of being told the truth. In sessions the mother began to work very painfully through her feelings of guilt which for a long time had been suppressed. She began to grieve appropriately for the child. At the same time she was unable to continue 'living a lie' with her own mother, and chose her moment carefully to tell her the real story. She was shocked by the reaction – her mother indicated that she too had been suppressing her own awareness of her daughter's responsibility. They were able to begin mourning for the child together.

Reaction to the death/injury and subsequent events

Memories and perceptions of a deceased child, along with the quality of the sense of loss, provide powerful material for examining the parents' views of reality. Idealization, denial, self-pity, and guilt have been important themes in our cases involving children who have been killed. We have been unable to find any literature which describes a grieving process peculiar to parents who have killed their own children. However, Burton has described some reactions of parents whose children died through illness or accident (1974).

It is important to establish what grieving processes the parents have experienced. Denial and minimization of responsibility are likely to inhibit appropriate grieving; these will be easily identifiable in sessions. Some themes are clearly ominous – for example when parents continue to negate the importance of the child, or continue to view the child as a threat.

These dynamics were apparent in an assessment which occurred three years after the death of a child at the hands of both parents. The presentation of the couple throughout the assessment was passive–aggressive, the father obsequious, and the mother passive. The completed genograms of both adults demonstrated graphically their intensely unsatisfactory and frustrating childhood and early adulthood. From the beginning their relationship was heavily over-invested as each partner sought from the other immediate satisfaction of his or her extensive unmet needs. They began to lose their separate identities and merge their personalities as they united to retaliate against the disturbed child who increasingly threatened their relationship.

It was never clear who struck the fatal blow, but the dynamics of *failure to protect* were as predominant as the aggression. The major finding of the assessment work with this couple was how little their relationship had changed. They both continued to deny responsibility for the extensive injuries which caused the child's death. Most significantly, the father still demonstrated feelings of anger towards the deceased child for 'getting in the way'.

The operation of the family system at the time of a child's death or serious injury is of crucial significance. Such families have simultaneously produced two sets of dangerous transactions: (a) the transaction of assault between perpetrator and victim; (b) the 'failure to protect' – *lack of action* – by the parent who is not the aggressor. In our experience, serious and fatal child abuse is rarely a simple transaction between one adult and one child. In addition to the classic aggressor–victim transaction, a crucial role is played by the other parent who is aware of acute danger, but fails to protect the child. The failure-to-protect role is at least as vital and pathological as that of the aggressor, but is often unrecognized as such by agencies who may collude unintentionally with an exclusive focus on the aggressor.

During the assessment, a clarification of the transactions behind the injury provides an important base-line against which to view changes in the operation of the family system.

Sentence and custody experiences

It is useful to explore the effects of discovery, questioning, arrest, trial, sentence, and associated publicity. What was the effect on the parents' relationship of these dramatic developments and of separation if prison sentences were imposed? Do the parents think their sentences were appropriate? If not, why not?

We have observed a range of reactions from parents who have

completed their sentences: one mother felt her sentence had not been long enough (four years' imprisonment) to reflect the seriousness of what she had done. One father, in contrast, was rather smug at having avoided a conviction for murder.

Prison experiences can be significant, particularly in promoting a gradual development of acceptance of responsibility for events, together with a greater understanding of their implications. It is not unusual for this process to be associated with religious experiences. In assessments it is more likely to be women who report that their prison experience was positive, perhaps in consequence of the significant differences between the regimes of men's and women's prisons in Britain.

Current pregnancy and current attitudes to children

We have found on more than one occasion that parents who have been convicted for child abuse have not been made aware that their sentence following conviction is not the end of the matter. Several families have conceived further children without knowledge of the child-care law under which subsequent children may be taken away from them if this is considered necessary for their protection. It would be helpful if courts at the time of conviction would routinely inform all adults found guilty of a Schedule 1 offence of the long-term implications.

In respect of the current pregnancy, two significant questions should be asked: why? and why now? Again there are parallels with parents who have lost a child in other circumstances. A range of motives and feelings including the wish to replace the lost child, and the need to make amends, may apply.

The team will explore the parents' general perception of the age-appropriate needs and abilities of children, including their knowledge of, and expectations and attitudes towards, child development. What are their current views regarding past mistakes? What has changed in their understanding of and attitudes to children? What do they intend to do differently? What else needs to change?

Spouse relationship: Review

We continue to pay close attention to the spouse relationship at all stages of the assessment – in our experience, the quality of the spouse relationship is crucial: *if the spouse relationship is not viable in a family where serious child abuse has occurred, then neither is the family*.

The team has by now worked with the couple through a large number of sessions in which contentious issues have been faced; what is the team's view of the parents' understanding of their relationship at the time of injury, and the ways in which it has since changed? What is the quality of the present relationship between the parents and the therapists?

In cases where progress is being made, there is likely to be an atmosphere of straightforwardness on both sides; and a wide range of interactional techniques – confrontation, empathy, teasing, and humour – will be brought into play as the family works on tasks. Parents will have grasped the opportunity presented by the structure of the assessment to disentangle themselves from their fights with agencies. They will have begun working energetically on the painful issues and difficulties within the family which they had previously avoided.

In cases where little progress has been made, the therapeutic system may be characterized by continuing tension and lack of trust between the parents and the therapists. It is crucial for the team to deal with the processes involved; and to do so invariably provides significant information so long as the therapists avoid being drawn into a *conflict-avoiding* response. The conflict must be explored – *the team should never lose sight of the possibility that the parents (or one of the parents) are passing a covert message that it would not be safe for the child to return home*.

The atmosphere may be one of sullenness or lack of energy on the part of the parents. The team may feel that the parents are 'jumping through hoops' by co-operating in attending sessions whilst demonstrating no commitment towards change. Sometimes the parents continue to attend in this mood for as long as the team offers appointments, so that their 'co-operation' can be presented to a court as evidence in favour of their child's return at a future revocation application.

When the team feels 'stuck' in such situations, it can be

productive to approach the resistance in a variety of different ways. The use of written 'homework' tasks may produce a significant response, and can be a very useful means of obtaining emotional feedback from verbally inarticulate or highly controlled personalities. Homework may illustrate the emotional intensity of parents who remain unable or unwilling to express such feelings spontaneously or verbally.

An example of this occurred in an assessment which followed a serious and unexplained injury to a young child. Several sessions had taken place at which the therapists attempted to counter the mother's passive–aggressive resistance. She attended all sessions punctually and politely. However, she presented as an emotional enigma, and refused the therapists any contact with her tightly controlled feelings. She did respond to a request to do some writing and brought the following material addressed to the therapists:

> 'These thoughts may not be what you want, but with me writing things like this, it makes me feel better, because I can put the hate I have for you on paper instead of keeping them inside. . . . I am a hard person . . . I have to be hard because of what I have been through in the past eight years, because if I showed my true feelings, people would see that I am a very unhappy person, and start feeling sorry for me and I would hate that, so that's why I wear a painted smile, I have all the feelings a person should have, because if I didn't I wouldn't be normal, I have love for my children, love for my mother, love and hate for M [boyfriend], and hate for you two, you wanted to know if I have feelings, well I can tell you they are there alright. . . .
>
> It's not just talk when I say I get angry, but I don't use it on people, like I can get all my anger out just by writing all this for you and the feelings I have for you which is hate – yes I can come to see you, all smiles and talk nice, but underneath I hate the sight of you.'

The feeling of the team working with this mother was frustration at being unable to engage her therapeutically in the assessment work. Because of this, and the lack of explanation for the original injury, it was not possible to return the child home.

During assessments parental *ambivalence* about the future of the child often becomes a significant area of work. Ambivalence may appear in different ways. It may be that from an early stage the parents openly express their doubts about their feeling for and commitment to the child, or it may be that such doubts emerge during the assessment work. On the other hand, it may be – as in the example of the mother just quoted – that the team has a firm hypothesis regarding parental ambivalence but this is verbally denied. However, the parents' behaviour often suggests otherwise. This may be most marked in cases where parents continually insist on their commitment to the child, but fail to take up opportunities to visit him or her regularly.

When the team suspects a denied ambivalence, it may be useful to introduce the child into assessment sessions at an early stage. Observations may then follow confirming the possibility of a lack of attachment, lack of parental interest in the child, and low frustration tolerance. Such parents often have an idealized vision of their relationship with the child, and such sessions allow the therapists to work with the parents (perhaps using videotape replays) along more realistic lines.

It is not uncommon that during such sessions the whole tone of the assessment task changes from 'Will *they* let us have the child back?' to 'Do *we* really want the child back?' A move into a stage of ambivalence in such circumstances may represent very positive progress from the original stance of idealization; the therapists need to be patient and to allow the process to assume its own direction. It is *not* necessarily the case that parents who begin to express ambivalent feelings for the first time in the assessment are moving towards a permanent separation from the child. In many of our cases of successful rehabilitation, the emergence of the feelings of ambivalence was the key to an effective therapeutic intervention which culminated in a firm, positive commitment to the child. Self-doubt precedes belief.

Other parents are already far more conscious of their feelings of basic ambivalence. They may work poignantly at this stage to form their own judgement of what would really be best for their child in the long term. Such dynamics tend to take one of two forms. A parent may come to recognize a basic rejection of the child which lay behind the injury or the failure to protect. The parent may use sessions to attempt to explain this to the spouse or significant other family members. This may create considerable crisis and recrimination in the family, or it may promote a sense of relief. In the second dynamic, the parent may reach the understanding that his or her own unmet personality needs are so great that he or she cannot provide any long-term, satisfactory parenting for the child, particularly when there is also an acknowledgement of a propensity for explosive violence when under pressure from the needs of others.

Whole-family sessions

Whole-family sessions may occur at any point during an assessment, or they may take place following a long period of work with the parents when rehabilitation is considered by the team to be a firm possibility. If rehabilitation is not feasible, then the reasons for this will be explained to the parents and the assessment will end with a recommendation to the local authority that the children do not return home.

In whole-family sessions a whole range of interactions can be observed through the use of simple tasks. We often ask families to prepare and eat a meal together under observation by the whole team. This task is in fact a sequence of many tasks involving several different simultaneous activities. It can be very valuable in providing a 'snap-shot' of family life and relationships presenting a microcosm of family strengths and weaknesses. The parental anxiety which the task invariably creates is useful as it intensifies feelings which are already present within the family. As a result, strengths and weaknesses which have already been identified from work with the parents in earlier sessions are often magnified and identified clearly as issues requiring further attention.

Feeding is a peculiarly crucial issue in family life and provides the basis for conflict between parents and children no matter what their ages. The preparation of appropriate food for others, and their acceptance and consumption of it, are extremely complex transactions requiring emotional consistency and commitment on both sides. It is clear from the range of childhood conditions involving some form of feeding disorder – from the baby who fails to thrive to the teenager with anorexia nervosa – that these reflect family relationships which have gone seriously wrong.

Feeding difficulties are commonly reported by parents who have abused their children. Powerful emotions are stimulated as parents experience their child's rejection of their best efforts. When this develops into physical abuse, it invariably means that the matter has become a serious power struggle between parent and child. The parent is likely to have adopted 'solutions' such as force-feeding, which have themselves intensified the problem. The parents' frustration may connect with unfinished business from their own unsatisfying experiences as children, and a historical, suppressed rage is unleashed. In child-abusing families, children's *normal* patterns of eating (including experiments with self-assertion through food refusal) provoke disproportionately intense negative emotional reaction in parents.

In addition to relationships specifically focused on food, the task of making and eating a meal also brings up a much wider range of issues. How organized are the parents in their preparations? How do they cope with preparing the meal *and* looking after the children at the same time? Do the parents work co-operatively through the simultaneous tasks, or do they become immobilized by arguments?

Meal times offer a good opportunity for observing how a family relates on issues such as encouragement and control. Of course in this unusual context, most parents are anxious for their children to eat the meal provided, for fear that the team might make a critical interpretation of their failure to do so. This anxiety gives the team a direct view of how the parents operate under pressure. Do they gently encourage or cajole the children? Do they plead or demand, or do they threaten the children? Are they bothered at all? Which parent takes responsibility? Does anyone remember to feed the baby?

The role of siblings can provide surprising and important information in such sessions. In a case where a five-year-old girl and a two-year-old boy were in care, predominantly because of physical neglect, towards the end of the assessment a session was held at which the parents prepared a meal for the family. During the eating of the very adequately prepared meal, it was obvious that the mother was totally unaware that the two-year-old needed to be helped and encouraged to eat at least a little of the adult-size portion he had been given. The stepfather seemed to have some awareness that a parental response was necessary, but seemed to have no realization that this could come from him. The intervention came from the five-year-old girl who seemed to realize that her brother should be eating something, and that she would need to lend a hand. When she did so, and with her assistance he began to eat, both parents allowed this to continue without any indication that they could take a part. The five-year-old's self-appointed role as 'little mother' continued immediately after the meal as *she* became aware of the need for a nappy change and began to undress her brother.

All sorts of similar examples relating to parental awareness, competence, motivation, control, affection, attachment, etc. can be produced by observation of simple tasks in family sessions. The use of the one-way screen can be important as it prevents the family from drawing the therapists in and so contaminating the dynamics, and also restrains the therapists from spontaneously intervening even when the baby appears to be drowning in spaghetti!

In many families where sexual abuse of a child has occurred it is often clearly demonstrated in assessments that there are severe communication problems within the family. Inhibited communication may be a fundamental feature of the dynamics of sexual abuse as the victim is unable to form a *protective alliance* with the non-abusing parent; instead he or she is coerced into keeping the abuse a secret.

Assessments of sexually abusing families follow a similar pattern to that outlined in this chapter, although the team is likely also to include simultaneous individual therapy with each parent and the victim. In general (but not always), victims of sexual abuse tend to be considerably older than victims of physical abuse; victims of sexual abuse always need individual therapy. The major therapeutic aim of work with the whole family is for the perpetrator to take *responsibility* for the abuse and to give a clear message to the victim that it was not his or her fault. Such families often find it particularly difficult to give clear messages as their communication channels tend to be blocked and distorted in an intense emotional atmosphere of suspiciousness and projection.

A useful technique for beginning to focus on communication in whole-family sessions is that of 'drawing a body'. The family as a whole are set the task of drawing a full-length body which includes all the visible sexual organs. The therapist may choose which sex the body should be according to the particular issues within each family, or the family may be left to decide themselves what sex it should be. Alternatively, two bodies, one of each sex, may be drawn. The family may have great difficulty in approaching this superficially simple task, and may get 'stuck' at several levels. It may be that they cannot decide who should initially take the most embarrassing role – that of actually doing the drawing. The dynamics of how this decision is resolved will be an indicator of general family functioning. It is not uncommon for both parents to look to the victim to take the lead.

As the drawing develops, information will be gleaned as to how the family communicates, or inhibits communication, about sexual matters. What is the role of sexuality within the family? What is the general knowledge about sexuality within the family? Many sexually abusing families operate through a total denial of sexuality on a verbal level – it is simply not spoken about.

To explore covert communication, and to promote overt communication, it is useful to extend the task once the body has been drawn to include a 'brainstorming' of different names for the various sexual parts. The role of each family member as to processes of inhibition will become clear. From this exercise it is possible to establish an agreed vocabulary for sexual parts of the body which of course will be talked about in detail in later sessions. It is only by spending a period of time on developing communication channels that family members can be freed to talk openly about significant issues.

Whole-family sessions often take place at the stage of an assessment when the team has virtually decided to make a recommendation for the children to be returned home to the care of their natural parents. Such sessions are vital in establishing to what degree the historical problems are still evident, what new problems have developed, and which specific issues will require further therapeutic work in the rehabilitation period.

At the final stage of the assessment, when the family is aware of the plan to return the children home, sessions can focus specifically on anticipated difficulties which may occur after their return. This also marks the beginning of the rehabilitation phase of intervention which is described in Chapter 7.

Individual therapeutic work with children

Many cases of serious child abuse involve very young children for whom the provision of a safe and nurturing environment is the prime therapeutic intervention during the period of the assessment. However, in cases where children are of an age to express consciously their feelings of confusion, uncertainty, and hurt about their experiences, it is essential that individual therapeutic work with them should take place.

The child needs to work consistently with the same therapist to whom he or she can learn to express a range of feelings in safety, and on whom he or she can depend for a consistent and appropriate level of understanding of past events and future possibilities. The therapist will use a range of techniques to make contact with the child's internal world, and many of these will depend on the use of symbols. Play materials including dolls, play people, plasticine, drawings, water, and candles are simple yet crucially effective in communicating with emotionally damaged children whose feelings so often are inaccessible at a verbal level.

Such work is fundamental in the case of abused children who are of an age to express important feelings (which are often ambivalent) as to whether or not they want to return home.

Decision-making

In order to make a recommendation for rehabilitation following serious child abuse, the team will require a clear understanding of the transactions of the original incident of abuse. This will include an understanding of the role of each family member, together with a clear perception of changes which have occurred in those relationships. An essential requirement of rehabilitation therefore is that the circumstances of the injury have been understood, and have changed. The team must feel that there is security about levels of physical safety, and appropriate physical and emotional developmental progress.

However, besides these fundamental requirements, many families will continue to experience a range of difficulties which are not in themselves sufficient to prevent rehabilitation. The goal is not to resolve every problem or difficulty which the family experiences; we would expect few of our families to be problem-free in rehabilitation. Indeed the process of returning children home from foster care will invariably raise difficulties regarding their reintegration into their natural families once an initial 'honeymoon' stage has come to an end. In many cases it is at this point that a great deal of further productive therapeutic work can be done. Following rehabilitation, families are viewed as ex-child-abusing families who now have an increased ability and motivation to resolve their continuing difficulties in more appropriate ways.

Disagreements

Particular care will need to be taken when the team cannot agree as to whether or not rehabilitation is feasible. In a cohesive and experienced team, although disagreements and different hypotheses will often be in the air during various stages of the assessment, it is unusual for these not to be resolved into a unanimous decision about the future of the children. In most cases by the end of such an intensive process the correct recommendation has become obvious to the team and in many cases to the parents as well.

In cases where the team continues to have different views about a recommendation, it is vitally important for it to take 'time out' to review what is happening in its internal processes to prevent agreement being reached. It may be that a mirroring process is occurring, perhaps with splits within the team reproducing similar splits between family members. The subtle and insidious effect of such processes should not be underestimated. The team must make time to examine each member's part in this process, and a high degree of personal openness and emotional honesty will be required. Often it can be productive to use an outside consultant to deal with the team's 'stuckness' over an especially difficult case. We have described elsewhere such a case of 'stuckness' in respect of our own team processes during work with a sexually abusing family (Dale *et al.* 1986).

Decisions

There can be no simple equation for balancing the pros and cons of the alternatives available for children in care following serious abuse. Such decisions have tremendous implications for the child's future life, identity, and personality, and are perhaps the most awesome within the sphere of the social work profession. There is a minefield of dilemmas for practitioners, and considerable temptation to avoid decisions altogether.

It is now abundantly clear – as many adults who have grown up in care will testify – that *no decisions are the worst decisions*. To 'drift' in 'care' over a long period of time without a plan for a permanent family placement (either through rehabilitation or through adoption) has exceptionally pernicious and irremediable effects.

If abused children and their siblings cannot return home in safety within a reasonable period of time, then an alternative permanent family placement must be provided. It is crucial that such decisions be taken carefully in the light of the best information and advice available; that they be primarily child-focused; that they be taken in good faith; and that they be open to examination in the courts.

CHAPTER 6

Case study

Introduction

Dangerous families exist within a social context which itself often unintentionally promotes and sustains the dynamics of risk within the families. In the book so far, we have described the operation and significance of five *systems* which interweave around families and professionals. These five systems can be viewed in order of increasing size:

1. Family system
2. Therapeutic system
3. Team system
4. Inter-agency system
5. Family–agency system

We have stressed that dangerousness lies not only within family systems, but also within professional 'helping' relationships (the therapeutic system), within professional teams, and within multi-professional and agency relationships. We have proposed the formation of the family–agency system, through the convening of network meetings, as a means of intervention when processes within the other four systems have become ineffective and stuck.

This chapter follows the progress of a case in which a baby was considered to be at acute risk from the starting-point of the initial case-conference. Aspects of family and professional dangerousness operate simultaneously, and the effect of interventions into each of the five systems over a period of time is described.

Initial case-conference (month one)

The NSPCC team first heard of Sandra through chairing a

case-conference requested by her probation officer who was acutely concerned about the safety of her month-old baby. Such anxieties were fuelled by observations of her handling of her cat – when it was passive she would indulge it with a rather smothering affection; when it made any demands Sandra would respond aggressively and violently. The result was 'a very confused animal'.

The probation officer's fear that the baby would be subjected to similar extremes of behaviour proved to be correct. Sandra's initial handling of baby Jeremy (full-term, normal delivery) was inconsistent and ambivalent. Descriptions were given of mother handling the baby 'like a doll', being unpredictably over-attentive and then dismissive of him; feeding and sleeping difficulties quickly developed.

In Jeremy's early weeks, Sandra expressed satisfaction with his sleeping as much as thirteen hours at a time, and then taking only one ounce of milk. Her view was that the baby – who was always immaculately clean in his cot – was 'growing whilst asleep'. On occasions the health visitor would find the baby like this in the cot, but quite cold. On other occasions he would be sweltering, submerged beneath seven or eight blankets.

It was also apparent to the probation officer and the health visitor that Sandra became alarmingly agitated when the baby cried, and that she interpreted this as a criticism of herself as a mother. Sandra had reported squeezing the baby's face hard when he was a few weeks old, but no marks had been found. These concerns were enhanced by her obsessionality and over-cleanliness which were already affecting her regime with Jeremy.

Background

The case-conference decided to view these unusually acute concerns in the context of available information about Sandra's family background and current relationships.

It was known that Sandra had given birth to her first child, Robert, when she was still a schoolgirl, that he was now aged six, and that he was being brought up in the legal custody of a relative. Sandra had experienced a disturbed childhood in her family of origin, in which relationships appeared to have been chaotic with a succession of stepfathers. From the age of nine, Sandra had become an increasingly disturbed and difficult child, manifesting truancy and severely self-destructive behaviour. She was the victim of intra-familial sexual abuse at the age of twelve, which resulted in a prison sentence for the perpetrator. After his release from prison, he returned home but no statutory action was taken by the authorities to protect Sandra from him. She left home of her own accord and quickly became pregnant with Robert. In recent months she had obtained her tenancy in a multi-storey block of flats, and was maintaining an explosive and unpredictable relationship with her boyfriend David. David was Jeremy's father but did not live in their home. Sandra had little known contact with her family of origin.

Sandra's relationships are expressed diagrammatically in *Figure 1*.

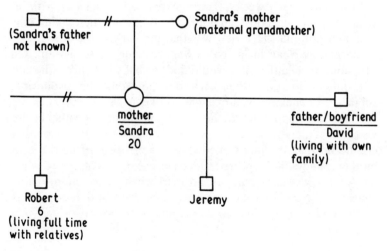

Figure 1   Sandra's genogram

Case-conference discussion

The conference felt that although the baby had as yet suffered no observable injury or neglect, there was considerable risk to his physical safety. The view expressed by the social services department was that notwithstanding this high risk, there were no legal grounds for taking the baby into care.

The conference was very well aware of the large gaps in significant information, particularly regarding Sandra's psychiatric history. Further anxiety was pooled – the probation officer disclosing her fantasy of Sandra hurling the baby out of the seventh-storey window of the flats. A comment was made that Sandra had 'stepped right out of a text-book'.

Although agency support for Sandra and baby was already at a high level, consideration was given to requesting a place for them at a newly opened Family Centre run by a voluntary social work agency. The conference decided to reconvene in four weeks time. In the meantime members would pursue the Family Centre referral, and obtain the missing information from other agencies.

Second case-conference (month two)

The second meeting was held on schedule and included two workers from the Family Centre which Sandra and Jeremy had already started attending. Sandra had continued to speak openly to the probation officer of worrying incidents involving the baby, including an occasion when she had flung him down on the bed in a temper. She had added that it could just as easily have been the floor. The probation officer commented that Sandra had now – uncannily – started talking of her own fear of throwing the baby through the window.

The family doctor had confirmed the psychiatric history from the age of nine. Sandra had seen a number of psychiatrists in several settings, but received little formal treatment. The only consistency between the various psychiatric opinions was that she was not psychotic.

The Family Centre workers described their initial impressions of Sandra. They saw her as a tense girl, who tried hard to appear to be coping, whilst not really believing it herself. She was already causing great concern by some aspects of her behaviour with Jeremy at the Centre. Her obsession about cleanliness had been strongly apparent, and she had been observed tipping the baby upside down when he was regurgitating so that he would not dirty his clothes.

The social services department had obtained more information about previous agency involvements with her family when Sandra was a child. In fact there had been contact with a large number of social work, special educational, and psychiatric agencies. Sandra's first self-injury was reported when she was seven; it was a self-inflicted wound requiring forty-eight stitches. Bizarre self-injuring episodes continued throughout her childhood, associated with moods of depression, withdrawal, and silence. Sandra presented all the signs and symptoms of a child who was being sexually abused, but the professional network at the time failed to recognize this.

The response of the case-conference to such information was anger at professional inaction to protect Sandra when she was a child, and pessimism about the future. However, the workers in direct contact with her felt that even with such a horrendous childhood Sandra seemed to possess many positive qualities which could be the focus for therapeutic work. Sandra was committed to attending the Family Centre, and was quite open about her difficulties. Most of the time the baby's demeanour was placid and manageable, and there was a general impression of good mothering most of the time. The case-conference concluded with the recognition that Sandra and Jeremy were settling into attendance at the Family Centre; and that this seemed to offer hope of therapeutic progress.

Third case-conference (month six)

The third conference was arranged at the request of the Family Centre workers as a matter of urgency, four months later. They reported a period of escalating concern, and revealed that they were now acutely worried about Jeremy's safety in Sandra's care. They described how Sandra had been extremely tense at the Centre the previous week, and had been loudly commenting that she was fed up with Jeremy and was going to give him something to make him ill so that he would be taken into hospital and she would be able to get her house tidy. She added – during the afternoon – that Jeremy had not had a feeding bottle since early the previous evening. Soon afterwards he was sick and Sandra yanked him away to change his nappy, which was in an unusually neglected condition.

This build-up of tension had culminated with Jeremy being very unhappy and unsettled, and Sandra responding to his crying by holding his face up to hers and bellowing in his face at the top of her voice: 'SHUT UP'. The baby had immediately gone silent and for some time afterwards appeared to be in a state of shock. The Centre workers obtained an urgent appointment with the family doctor who found the baby to be completely unresponsive and floppy. The doctor was unable to rouse him, and in addition noted that he was somewhat dehydrated. He insisted on hospital admission.

Although the hospital staff were made aware of the history of concern surrounding this baby, neither the hospital nor the Family Centre workers referred to the statutory child-care agencies (the social services department and the NSPCC child-protection team) before discharging Jeremy home to the care of his mother three days later. Since that time, Sandra had continued to make alarming statements about her attitude towards Jeremy. She had also become preoccupied with violent thoughts about her boy-friend, and talked enthusiastically about her attempts to harm him.

It was difficult to judge how accurate Sandra's reports of such incidents were. Certainly, David had made no complaint to the probation officer with whom he was in contact. However, David had described a statement of Sandra's to the effect that she was allowed to do anything at the Family Centre – including stabbing the baby – and that she would still be supported. The probation officer reported that she had become increasingly frustrated in her efforts to work with Sandra and David, and that her concern about Jeremy's safety was now greater than ever. The conference included a new health visitor who had become involved because Sandra had by this time been rehoused in a different area. Her observations were that Jeremy continued to develop normally and appeared to be well cared for. However, she was finding Sandra a very difficult mother to get through to and understand.

The Family Centre workers commented that they felt they were sitting on a 'time bomb'. Because of their acute concern for Jeremy's safety they had extended their role, and were virtually taking shifts at Sandra's home, even in the evenings and at weekends.

Case-conference dynamics

From the chairman's point of view, this meeting had all the characteristics of the 'stuck case-conference'. The longer the meeting went on, the more examples of 'acute concern' were pooled in a mounting spiral of anxiety. The chairman attempted to clarify the options open to the various agencies, and commented on the danger that Sandra's testing-out behaviour and threats of violence would prove self-fulfilling prophecies. It was agreed that Jeremy appeared to be in great danger, and there was a tentative acceptance of the chairman's view that Sandra was communicating covertly and desperately in an attempt to get the agencies to act to protect Jeremy from her.

The view of the social services department remained that there was still insufficient evidence on which to base a compulsory removal of Jeremy into care, either through a place of safety order, or through wardship proceedings.

The conference rebounded from this issue of legal 'stuckness' to become embroiled in other unresolvable issues. The different workers directly involved appeared to be following competing therapeutic models, which had the overall effect of cancelling one another out. The inter-agency system 'in action' in this conference provided an illustration of the complex web of covert agendas 'under the table' interfering with apparent problem-'solving' activity 'above the table'. The harder everyone worked to maintain their particular position – of style and degree of intervention (including non-intervention) – the more anxious and stuck the meeting became.

This case-conference occurred at a time when the team was developing the use of network meetings as a means of intervention when the inter-agency system was 'stuck'. The chairman suggested to the conference that as it was agreed that Sandra should be clearly informed of the level of professional anxiety regarding her care of Jeremy, a network meeting would be the appropriate forum for this statement to be made.

The basic format of network meetings was described in Chapter 2; they represent an outside 'meta' intervention into the family–agency system. A member of the team with no previous involvement with the management of the case acts as convenor to the existing family and agency grouping.

Network meeting two weeks later (month six)

Typically, the professionals were rather more anxious than the family. The spontaneous seating diagram is shown in *Figure 2*. The meeting lasted two hours and some of the significant events will be described. The initial *verbal round* gave the opportunity for each professional to describe his/her specific role. The *senior social worker* said her responsibility was to help families who had problems in coping with their lives. On behalf of the local authority she had legal power to protect children who were in danger.

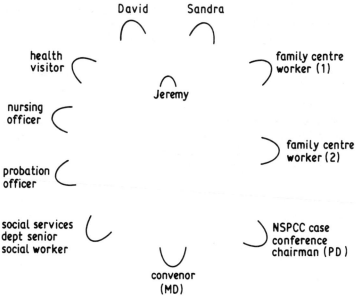

Figure 2   Sandra's network meeting

The *probation officer* said that through the probation order she had a duty to 'advise, assist, and befriend' Sandra. The *nursing officer* said that she had supervisory duties in respect of the work of the health visitor. The *health visitor* said that she had a responsibility for monitoring Jeremy's development. The *Family Centre workers* said that their role was to support families who were struggling with difficulties. The *NSPCC team member* said that one of his roles was to chair case-conferences when concern was felt about children, and that he was doing so with this family. Another role was to provide advice to other professionals working with families; another was to work directly with families where children had been removed to see whether the difficulties could be resolved and the children returned.

The *second round* of '*What is your problem?*' began to reveal rather more significant processes. Notwithstanding the discussion which had taken place in the three recent case-conferences, the *senior social worker* felt that she had no problem with this family. The *probation officer* felt that she was not sure that she had a problem either. She wanted to ensure that 'support' was around for Sandra at times when the Family Centre staff were unavailable. The *nursing officer* felt that she did not have any problems. The *health visitor* reported that she had only recently become involved with Sandra, who initially had maintained that she did not want a health visitor. However, there were no problems with Jeremy's development, and Sandra co-operated with clinic attendances.

David felt that his problem was with Sandra's mother, whom he described as being a bad influence on her. *Sandra* spoke at length about her problem, focusing mainly on David: 'I want him to go but he won't go . . . when he does go, I want him back . . . when he doesn't do as I tell him I scream at him and when he does do what I say I still scream at him.' This culminated with: 'I take it out on *him* [Jeremy], to get at *him* [David].'

The *Family Centre* workers said that their problems centred on their anxiety about Sandra's behaviour when she was tense: 'You play games with the baby that frighten the pants off us.' *Sandra* smiled her agreement, saying that she would pretend to 'bounce Jeremy against the wall . . . but I never dropped him.'

The *NSPCC team member* said that he had a big problem: having chaired three case-conferences he was aware that the professionals had other concerns which they had not been open about in this meeting. He had been very worried about the descriptions given in the case-conferences about the relationship between Sandra and Jeremy, and the prospect that he could be seriously injured. He was concerned that the professionals could express these concerns to him, but not to Sandra herself.

Sandra responded: 'They should be truthful, shouldn't they?'

Sculpting

Time allowed for the sculpting of the family–agency network from two perspectives: firstly Sandra's and then David's.

Sandra's sculpt

Sandra began by selecting the person in the room to whom she felt closest, Jeremy, and removing him from David's knee in the process. The person of next greatest significance to her was the probation officer whom she caricatured as talking a great deal in 'advising' her – the appropriate physical posture being: 'Just one great big mouth!' The two Family Centre workers she placed in equally close proximity, and the convenor pressed her to demonstrate how they were different. Initially they had to juggle to stand on the same spot, but Sandra refined this to have one focusing on herself, and the other concentrating on Jeremy.

Sandra experienced the physical closeness of the sculpt as intolerable, and she would not let any of the professionals touch her. In her sculpted position of being almost submerged by an overpowering group of professionals, she felt physically uncomfortable and pushed them away. Sandra needed more space.

David's sculpt

There were two significant features of David's sculpt, one immediately apparent: *he* held Jeremy. Secondly, he pulled all the professionals directly back into close physical proximity around Sandra, leaving himself and Jeremy on the outside. He saw himself and Jeremy as being separate from Sandra – *her* 'problems', and *her* 'helpers'.

Written exercise

The *senior social worker* offered voluntary reception into care for Jeremy. Sandra and David were united in declining this. The *probation officer* offered to help Sandra to become 'happier and more content', and to provide her with *more* support and friendship. This offer was accepted by Sandra. The *Family Centre* workers offered to continue their support. This was also accepted, as was the *health visitor*'s role of continuing to advise on Jeremy's development. The *NSPCC team member* offered a formal assessment of the family if Jeremy had to be taken into care on a statutory basis. Sandra noted this with interest but did not see it as being currently relevant.

Discussion

The network meeting has been briefly described from the individual perspectives of the professionals, but this does not present a picture of their interrelationship, nor of their inter-actions with the positions of Sandra and David. A vivid picture of family and family–agency relationships is gained in such meetings as much from non-verbal as from verbal behaviour in a way which is difficult to portray in written words.

From the meeting as a whole, the NSPCC team formed clear hypotheses about the over-involved and enmeshed positions of certain professional members of the network. There was a complete 'stuckness': the harder they worked, the worse Sandra became, causing them to work even harder. It was a classic vicious circle. From the professional standpoint of the enmeshed workers, the therapeutic hope was that Sandra's behaviour represented a severe 'testing-out' of their commitment, and that once they had demonstrated their *acceptance*, *trust* would develop, and Sandra's attitudes and behaviour would mature. On the other hand the health visitor was noted to be measuring her own involvement with great care, and was clearly not intending to be sucked into a similarly enmeshed position, although she did intend to monitor the child's development. This position was appropriately sup-ported by her manager. The senior social worker offered a 'solution' of a completely different kind which did not fit with any other of the therapeutic proposals, but which did fit the 'respite care' model of that particular team at that time.

A major feature of the professional group was the *clash of therapeutic models*. This was affected not only by agency orienta-tions, but by the personalities of each individual involved. There were widely differing views as to Sandra's needs – ranging from intensive and prolonged re-parenting, specific intra-psychic coun-selling, and conjoint sessions with David. At the other end of the continuum was a view that her behaviour was attention-seeking and manipulative, and that she was using Jeremy as currency to obtain and sustain the attention she was receiving from workers who had become emotionally over-involved.

The feeling of the team was that this had been a 'more of the same' network meeting, and that little change had occurred at it. Nevertheless, the previous network experience of the team indicated that the possibility of significant changes in the weeks ahead should not be excluded. Questions posed within the team centred on whether the enmeshed professionals would take steps to control the extent of their involvement or whether Sandra's behaviour would deteriorate to demand even more of their time.

Subsequent events

A short period of relative calm after the network meeting was followed by an intensification of tension and concern as Sandra again resumed her dramatic and threatening gestures towards Jeremy. Again the Family Centre workers and the probation officer were drawn into extended hours of surveillance and practical care-taking because of their reluctance to leave Sandra alone with Jeremy.

Eventually a neighbourhood fracas developed late one evening and the Family Centre workers and neighbours had to physically restrain Sandra who was in a drunken, hysterical state. Police involvement led to Sandra being taken to the local psychiatric hospital by ambulance, and the social services department (finally) intervening to obtain a place of safety order on Jeremy once it was established that there were no grounds for Sandra to be compulsorily detained in hospital under mental health legislation.

Fourth case-conference (month seven)

A further case-conference was convened to review the situation following Jeremy's dramatic admission into care. All the professionals directly involved expressed relief that the baby was now literally in a place of safety. The comment was made that the more they had tried to 'help' Sandra, the 'more diabolical she became'. The consultant psychiatrist presented his opinion that Sandra was not mentally ill, but had an explosive personality disorder; he shared the concerns expressed about the safety of the child. The conference was in no doubt of the need to pursue care proceedings on Jeremy with a strong recommendation to the court that a care order be made. The NSPCC would then offer Sandra a period of assessment and work towards a recommendation regarding Jeremy's future.

Some reservations were expressed about the exact state of 'hard' evidence to present to the juvenile court to support the recommendation of a care order. However, there was overall agreement that in situations such as this, considered by the professional group to be very dangerous, the child's safety should not be risked further by fears about whether the evidence would turn out to be adequate. It was stressed by the NSPCC team that care proceedings represented a new therapeutic approach geared around the imposition of limits, together with a firm statement to Sandra about the unacceptability of her behaviour. A care order need not be seen as the 'end', but as a new beginning for Sandra herself to review her relationship with Jeremy.

Subsequent events

Following the case-conference, Sandra was informed of the plan to obtain a care order on Jeremy; the NSPCC team, she was told, would work with her to assess whether Jeremy would be allowed to return to her care. Sandra's response was to express *relief* that her child was in care, and to indicate that she would not oppose the application for a care order provided that she could work with the NSPCC team to try to understand why things had gone so badly wrong.

Jeremy settled into a local foster home, and Sandra consistently and punctually attended for her twice-weekly access sessions.

Juvenile court

At the care proceedings, Jeremy's father (David) had indicated that he would pursue his own legal action to obtain custody of Jeremy. He did not want the child to be in Sandra's care or in the care of the local authority. However, in the care proceedings the court rejected his application to be made a party to the proceedings. The court accepted the application by the local authority for a care order on the basis of the child's 'proper development being avoidably prevented or neglected' (*see* 'primary grounds for care proceedings', p. 53). Sandra did not contest the application for a care order on the basis that she would then take part in the assessment work with the NSPCC team.

The assessment

A firm principle of the NSPCC team during statutory assessments is to request the withdrawal or reduction of involvement by other agencies during the period of work. Following the care order it is important to clarify what each individual agency's role will be. In this case it was agreed that it would not be appropriate for the Family Centre workers to continue their intensive, nurturing contact with Sandra, as this would clash with the NSPCC team's plan to explore how much responsibility the 'adult' Sandra could take for herself. It was agreed that Sandra would still be invited to various 'social' aspects of the Family Centre's activity. The probation officer stated that she would have no contact with Sandra during the period of the assessment.

When the care order was made, it was learned that Sandra was three months pregnant. It was agreed that the task of the assessment would be to recommend not only about Jeremy's future, but also about whether there would be any need for statutory action when the new baby was born. It was agreed that the health visitor's role during the assessment would be minimal because the child was in care, but Sandra would need her advice about ante-natal care.

The preliminary spadework of 'clearing the ring' is vital as it provides space for a more uncontaminated view of the family's own capabilities, as well as reducing (but not eliminating) the scope for inter-agency conflicts and manipulation.

Formation of the therapeutic team

At the request of the senior social worker, an '*ad hoc*' team was to be formed for this particular assessment. (Issues surrounding the formation of *ad hoc* teams were discussed in Chapter 4.) It is important to test the viability of the proposed team before work with the family begins. In this case, the social services department worker had previously been involved in succesful *ad hoc* teams. Following initial discussion, roles for this therapeutic team were clarified as: therapists – M.D. (NSPCC) and K.D. (SSD); consultant – P.D. (NSPCC).

The assessment took place over a period of four months (Months Ten to Fourteen) and involved fourteen sessions at the NSPCC unit. There were three distinct phases: (a) the first four sessions, concerned with engagement issues; (b) seven individual sessions, with a specific therapeutic focus; (c) three sessions with Sandra and Jeremy together.

Engagement

It was essential to clarify the role of David in respect of Sandra and the assessment. The first session involved both adults and demonstrated vividly their intention to prevent the other from having care of Jeremy; and the extent to which their relationship was negative and mutually provocative. David was adamant in his decision to pursue separate legal action: he was only prepared to attend sessions to compete with Sandra as an alternative parent. He made it clear that he did not consider that she could ever be an acceptable parent to Jeremy.

Sandra expressed her reluctance to have joint sessions with David: she wanted to work on her own difficulties and did not want him to be part of this as he was not committed to her and might use the material against her in the threatened legal proceedings. The team felt that it was important to begin the assessment work with Sandra alone, as David clearly preferred things to remain 'stuck', hoping to be able to move in and out of sessions as it suited him. He was defined out with Sandra's agreement.

Second session (M.D. and K.D., with P.D. consulting)

At the *pre-briefing* it was agreed that the session should focus predominantly on the 'here and now' processes within the room. Given Sandra's well-recognized skill at manipulation, and her experience of a wide range of previous therapeutic contacts, it was crucial to obtain a 'base-line' of her behaviour and attitude towards the team at the beginning of work, against which to measure future changes.

It quickly became evident that a 'therapeutic contest' of cup-tie proportions was in the offing. M.D. and Sandra became enbroiled in a battle around her refusal to estimate how many psychiatrists she had seen. Sandra used every opportunity to score critical points against previous 'helpers', e.g. 'The social workers when I was a child allowed me to be in and out of care – they should have sorted my Mam out before I went home.'

It was not possible to ignore the significance of Sandra's comments for *her* current position – her need to be 'sorted out' before Jeremy was allowed to return home. How hard would she be prepared to work? Would she merely expect the professionals to work hard to change her?

The therapists explored with Sandra another crucial process issue – that of her previous relationships with 'helpers'. Sandra acknowledged that she had always played a game with professionals who attempted to get close to her – 'by not letting them . . . and then they give up'.

> K.D. You're pleased when you prove people to be bad . . . you get satisfaction from that.
>
> SANDRA. People are bad . . . I don't know why.

Noting the process of Sandra's defeat of a succession of previous 'helpers', M.D. took the (strategically provocative) stance of anticipating that Sandra would be able to defeat this team as well. The value of strategic interventions with such skilful clients is demonstrated throughout this assessment. Sandra could not resist the challenge: 'How can you help me if you've got such a low opinion of yourself?' Tension became acute when M.D. made an anticipatory comment about the 'prickliness' the team would be expecting from Sandra during the assessment. Sandra reacted explosively and angrily, standing up to leave: '*You're* playing games . . . need to grow up. . . . *You're not going to beat me.*'

This was a straight demonstration of the underlying therapeutic contest which had dominated the session, and an overt statement of Sandra's power. However, importantly, the process of Sandra projecting her own internal battles on to the therapists – and then herself recognizing this – also became apparent:

SANDRA. I know you two only want what is best for Jeremy.

M.D. But in the back of your mind you feel we've already decided.

SANDRA. But *I* have got to want him back.

During a break, the consultant commented that Sandra was largely in control and even more expert at games than M.D. and K.D. together. The setting was very comfortable for her, and she was easily able to demonstrate her anti-therapeutic skills. Sandra was much less comfortable when she became fleetingly in touch with her internal ambivalences. The therapists had explained that one of the options at the end of the assessment would be for Jeremy to return home; this had caused Sandra discomfort. She would prefer to play 'victim' to a team who stated that Jeremy could not return home, rather than face the painful issues required for change. The session ended with Sandra being given the dates of a sequence of sessions, and informed that a contract for the assessment would be discussed during the next meeting.

Subsequent events

Immediately after this session, Sandra made contact with the Family Centre workers and complained angrily about the attitude of the NSPCC team – that they did not understand her as the Family Centre workers did. The Family Centre workers became drawn into this, and made several phone calls to the NSPCC team, asking them to try to reassure Sandra and calm her down. The team refused to do so, and this led to an atmosphere of mutual frustration and irritation between the two agencies. The team decided to postpone Sandra's next individual session, and to use the appointment instead for another meeting of the family–agency system. This would enable the renewed inter-agency differences, which Sandra both exposed and augmented, to be tackled further.

Second family–agency system meeting (third session, month eleven)

Following the principle of using 'meta' interventions into 'stuck' systems, the consultant requested another NSPCC team member

(J.W., who had no previous involvement in the case) to act as convenor for this meeting. It was important that the therapeutic team did not have responsibility for 'solving' the problem, but could use the session on the same level as the other parties to experience it, and in the same way be subject to the effects of the external intervention.

The convenor had no difficulty in directing the meeting to examine the 'here and now' processes, and the session quickly became tense, emotional, and productive. All members took the opportunity to reveal sources of irritation and frustration, and vulnerable feelings. Inter-agency myths and perceptions were finely examined:

M.D. strategically brought Sandra back into the centre of these issues: 'What do you think of us all, Sandra . . . arguing, not being able to sort ourselves out?' Sandra (showing again that she could not resist a challenge) answered 'I don't think that you all know what you're doing.'

The consultant and the convenor decided together that a task was required following the period of 'storming'. The task was given: the meeting had only thirty minutes to work together and alone to establish a mutually satisfactory set of relationships that would allow the assessment to proceed. The mood changed towards a cohesive group atmosphere which Sandra was fully participant in. The 'clearing of the air' produced a rapid 'clearing of the ring' as each person declared openly their position and expectation of all the other parties. Agreement was reached about Sandra's limited contact with the Family Centre: the workers would make no response to her 'crises' between sessions; and Sandra would not 'wind up' any other agencies during the assessment work.

Discussion

It was felt that the meeting had been therapeutically important for Sandra, apart from any spin-offs in inter-agency understanding. She had been attentive throughout, and remained energetic at the end when the professionals around her were flagging. She had clearly got the message that one of the expectations of the assessment work was that she control the provocative and manipulative aspects of her behaviour more consistently.

The team was less sure what her subsequent behaviour would be. It was possible that she might 'raise the stakes', and if so, given her repertoire of behaviour, literally anything could happen. On the other hand, there was the more distinct possibility that now Sandra's games had been openly 'named', she would settle down to do the assessment work. Her behaviour over the following days and weeks would be the only significant indicator of which way she was moving. This was Sandra's responsibility. The assessment had begun.

Fourth session (one week later)

K.D. was away sick – a significant but unwilled event. Consequently M.D. saw Sandra alone, with P.D. consulting. This was a crucial session, focusing on the assessment contract and arousing further covert resistance from Sandra.

Sandra's assessment contract

'1. The aim of the assessment is to make a recommendation about the future of Jeremy, and Sandra's unborn child.

2. The assessment period will be at least three months.

3. Sessions will take place weekly at the NSPCC Child Protection Team. Consultancy to the therapists will be provided by direct observations of sessions through a one-way screen. Sandra agrees to sessions being video-taped.

4. Sandra agrees to co-operate with the assessment which will look in detail at her background, previous relationships, and current family life and relationships.

5. Sandra's contact with previous helpers will be explored, as will her ability to live a mature, adult, independent existence.

6. The Family Centre, which previously provided therapeutic help, will during the period of the assessment now only offer opportunities for social activities and contact. Sandra is free to choose whether to use this or not.

7. Sandra has access to Jeremy at the foster home on Monday and Wednesday afternoons. If she needs to change these arrangements she will discuss this with the foster parents in advance. Sandra agrees to behave in a reasonable way at all times when she is in the foster home.

8. When necessary other extended family members may be asked to take part in sessions.

9. At some sessions Jeremy may also be present.

10. Sandra's bus fares to attend sessions and to visit Jeremy will be reimbursed.'

Sandra initially objected to the possibility that her mother could be asked to attend sessions, but as M.D. focused on the process of her disagreement, it gradually evaporated. After she had agreed with all the clauses in the contract, M.D. began to explore with Sandra the possible ways in which she might sabotage it. Suddenly and eagerly Sandra produced from her bag a photo of herself as a child, allowing M.D. to look at it for several seconds before equally suddenly snatching it back. The next thirty minutes of the interview focused solely on that incident, and a powerful 'therapeutic contest' was played out between the therapist and Sandra over his request that the photo should remain out on view for himself and the consultant behind the mirror.

It was clear, from the history, that the substance of the issue – Sandra being viewed and metaphorically touched – was very crucial to her. However, the *process* of her action – to reveal the photo (a bit of herself) and then to withdraw it – was at that stage of equal significance. The therapist focused solely on the process of withdrawal, and there was a long and tense impasse. The temptation in such circumstances is to 'give in' and evade the issue by switching to a mutually less contentious *content* issue; this was avoided. To avoid conflict, rather than explore it and identify openly the processes involved, amounts to a serious loss of therapeutic opportunity – although it undoubtedly leads to more comfortable sessions.

Change for Sandra began to occur:

M.D. The photos are an important measure of how much you will share . . . perhaps you need more time than we have today . . . you could put the photos on the desk . . . point them up towards the camera. [*His posture indicates that this is the only way out of this stuckness, and is something that Sandra will have to do.*]

SANDRA. I'd rather do something else.

M.D. [*shrugs*]. Yes, but it's my room.

SANDRA [*angrily*]. That's childish – 'It's my room' – It's not

your room at all.
[M.D. *laughs*.]

SANDRA [*angrily*]. Why do you laugh?

M.D. Sometimes people say things that amuse me . . . it felt like you were being a mother to me – telling me off . . . But seriously – it's more my room than it is yours.

SANDRA [*looks to argue*]. I thought you were going to ask me about David and Jeremy – you've never once asked about them.

M.D. We can have an argument if you want to, but that will only get us away from the very important issue of how much you are prepared to share . . . as you get angry – you may have a tantrum – go and wind up the Family Centre.

SANDRA. I'll use another way.

M.D. You'll have more ways than I can keep track of . . . I'll always struggle to keep up with you.

M.D. commented that the session had been 'very productive' and that he had noted a clear distinction between Sandra *saying* that she would be open, and her *behaviour* which did not match her words. Sandra responded angrily, getting all of the photographs out of her bag, flinging them on to the table, lighting a cigarette, and starting to cry. At that point the consultant rang through to suggest to the therapist that he focus on Sandra's *tears*, rather than her pictures. From that point onwards, the session – and indeed the whole assessment – began to reflect Sandra's genuine therapeutic engagement in the work as she attempted to make some sense of her history, identity, and behaviour. She had lost the power struggle in that session, but paradoxically had gained considerable freedom, by being divested of her traditionally controlling and manipulative relationship with 'helpers'.

Her mood changed significantly later in the same session as she spoke about Jeremy: 'I wanted him to be clean, polite, and happy – I knew when I was having him that it was wrong – I didn't feel love for him – not proper love – it was love for what I was going to make him, not for what he would be . . . I wouldn't give Jeremy back to anyone who behaved like me.'

De-briefing

Therapist and consultant both recognized the significance of this session. Through the therapeutic technique of constantly returning responsibility to Sandra and unremitting concentration on the conflictive nature of the process in the room, she had ultimately taken the significant decision to allow herself to take the risk of losing a fight, and to begin to share her feelings of powerlessness and vulnerability.

Again it was clear that her behaviour *after* the session would be of equal significance. The three possibilities seemed to be: (1) a return to aggressive manipulation of other agencies; (2) 'caving-in' behaviour – perhaps self-injury; (3) settling down into regular attendance at sessions, and developing the therapeutic experience she had just begun.

Seven 'engaged' individual sessions

Sandra settled down into 100 per cent attendance at sessions and at access meetings in the foster home; she ceased making demands on outside agencies. In the succeeding seven sessions the focus subtly but definitely shifted away from the question of: 'Will the team allow Sandra to have Jeremy back?' to a more fundamental question which acknowledged her struggle with her ambivalence: 'Does she consistently *want* him back?' By the end of the seven sessions (which were conducted by M.D. alone, K.D. joining P.D. as consultant) Sandra had covered enormous ground. She had experienced in sessions several cathartically painful and angry experiences as she relived certain events and relationships, particularly in respect of the background of sexual abuse.

The structure of the therapeutic team, providing constant (but usually unobtrusive) consultation, was a vital factor in enabling the therapist to maintain an increasingly warm but neutral therapeutic stance during intense and poignant sessions. It was Sandra's work, and she had to do it. The therapeutic team aimed to provide her with sufficient impetus (including at times firm challenges) to take emotional risks, without this pressure becoming persecuting. Similarly, it was a human response to be affected by her pain, but to 'rescue' her from it ultimately would not be helpful to her.

During these sessions Sandra developed the ability to experience her painful feelings rather than suppress them and substitute obsessional behaviour in their place. A picture began to emerge of a 'whole' Sandra, with a real, positive emotional core to her life; and Sandra began to see the possibility of becoming independent of her past. She began to take more appropriate and consistent control of the important relationships in her life – particularly with Jeremy, David, and her mother. Significantly – and this will not be a surprise to readers with family therapy experience – David and Sandra's mother did not take kindly to the changes in her which they experienced.

It was clear from work with Sandra on her family tree that her experience of sexual abuse as a child contained a store of unexpressed and unresolved confusing feelings for her. From a *Gestalt* perspective this represented important 'unfinished business' which continued to have an adverse effect on her experience of life and on her behaviour in relationships. The final two individual sessions were used to focus on this issue. The sessions spent on Sandra's experience of being sexually abused and of not being protected either by her family or by the agencies around it were a profound indictment of professional shortsightedness and dangerousness. She said: 'I'm annoyed – it could have been stopped and it wasn't . . . I told my teacher what he'd done and what I had to do – she didn't believe me – there was nobody to turn to except the teacher – they made her go to court because she never reported it.' We have given elsewhere a detailed account of therapeutic intervention with a sexually abusing family, including a discussion of the significant factors influencing the behaviour of the inter-agency system (Dale *et al.* 1986).

Team discussion

On several occasions in previous sessions, the hypothesis had been explored that Sandra's original bizarre behaviour had been geared towards Jeremy being removed from her, both in the short and the long term. It had been important to consider the idea that Jeremy's future could be with another family. Focusing on this possibility provided the context for Sandra to explore openly her ambivalence by considering all the available options. The possibility of an *agreed* permanent separation could not be ruled out at this stage.

In considering the potential for rehabilitation, it was important to be clear what changes were *essential* if Jeremy were to return home, as opposed to what changes would be merely desirable. It was felt at this stage that Sandra's settled behaviour, calmness, and consistency constituted the *essential* positive changes, and that it was not reasonable to expect that all of her remaining emotional and relationship difficulties (so long as these did not significantly affect Jeremy) be resolved as a condition of rehabilitation. Further work on these issues could be offered in a rehabilitation phase.

Out of this discussion came a recognition that the team had been discussing 'when' Jeremy would return home, rather than 'if' he would return. Having recognized this, the team quickly realized that his return 'home on trial' should be sooner rather than later, in view of the baby which was expected in three months time. It was felt that there would be little physical risk to Jeremy in Sandra's care. She had long since stopped playing her threatening, manipulative games using Jeremy as currency; moreover, if these recurred they would be instantly recognizable and their significance clear. In this situation, it was important to observe and explore Sandra's emotional reaction to the news that Jeremy's return home was to be recommended. Experience with other families had shown that the parental response to such news can be unpredictable. Fearful and rejecting feelings towards the child may suddenly recur at this point, particularly in parents who have overtly or covertly struggled with basic feelings of ambivalence towards the child. It has been known for parents who cannot acknowledge such feelings *verbally* to respond to the news of proposed rehabilitation with such behaviour as to bring the viability of the suggestion immediately back into question. Such reactions seem to represent a *covert* message that the child would not be safe if returned, or that he or she does not have a place within the family. Such reactions need to be explored very carefully and taken very seriously.

The team felt that the improvement in Sandra's relationship with Jeremy was too authentic for such a surprising response to be made in this case; nevertheless it was carefully watched for. Returning Jeremy before the new baby was born would give Sandra the time required to review her commitment to being a mother to the baby. She had been using sessions to explore actively her ambivalent feelings about the baby. This included looking at the possibility that following Jeremy's return she might feel that the care of two children was too demanding for her, that her commitment to Jeremy was her priority, and that the baby should be placed for adoption.

It was decided that the next three sessions should be attended by Sandra and Jeremy together so that their relationship and her parenting skills could be examined in more detail. This would be complementary to feedback and observations received throughout the assessment from her visits to the foster home.

Three sessions with mother and child (month fourteen)

By the time these sessions occurred, Jeremy was fourteen months old, and had spent exactly half his life in a foster home. The team felt that it would be useful for mother and child to spend the whole day together in the NSPCC Unit, although the session would not take place until the afternoon. Throughout the morning Sandra and Jeremy were left alone in a rather spartan room, with access to toilets and kitchen, but with little to occupy themselves. Such boredom creates a realistically stressful situation in which the team can observe parental ingenuity and skills.

Throughout the three sessions, Sandra demonstrated a degree of maternal skill, competence, confidence, and patience with Jeremy which took the team rather by surprise. There were several tantrums from an overtired Jeremy, which Sandra dealt with very appropriately. Sandra showed little sign of tension or frustration in this experience even though she was aware that she was being observed. Sandra was noted to be working hard on overcoming her over-cleanliness, and expressed far more realistic attitudes about Jeremy getting messy. She acknowledged that if her obsessionality again came to influence her behaviour and her handling of the children, then this would be a clear sign that she was again under considerable stress. She described how in the past she had exaggerated her obsessional and threatening behaviour in the presence of other professionals: 'I'd do daft things . . . I'd tip him up so he wouldn't be sick on me . . . I wouldn't hold him softly as a baby . . . I was rough with him . . . constantly changing his clothes . . . calling him "dirty" . . . but it was *normal* . . . and I felt that if I didn't treat him bad I wouldn't be allowed to go to the Centre . . . I treated him worse there than at home.'

Rehabilitation

Returning children 'home on trial' while still subject to care orders allows the local authority to insist on as many conditions as are felt necessary in the interests of their protection. Rehabilitation contracts as used by this team are often presented as the beginning of a second stage of assessment. This will usually be in the context of a view that the child will be basically safe in the care of the parent(s), but that problems do remain, usually connected with child-developmental issues and management. Often there is a feeling that such issues can only be resolved by continuing work with the family after the children are back in the home on a full-time basis. There is a limitation on therapeutic scope for dealing with parenting issues when the children are in care and exposed to different styles of parenting (i.e. natural and foster) simultaneously. The children's return home in such circumstances provides a significant test of natural parenting capabilities (and ability to use the help on offer), because the new move can be expected to provoke the child to display a fair amount of regressed or 'testing-out' behaviour. For parents, rehabilitation contracts offer the possibility of working towards their ultimate goal – revocation of the care order.

The use of rehabilitation contracts, and issues arising in this stage of work, are discussed in Chapter 7, where Sandra's rehabilitation contract is reproduced. At the point when the rehabilitation contract is agreed with the family, it is important that a case-conference be reconvened for the inter-agency system to hear and respond to the work and recommendation of the team.

Fifth case-conference (month fifteen)

The assessment work of the team was presented in detail to the multi-disciplinary group. The content of the work and the important processes observed were described, together with a statement of the significant changes made by Sandra. In addition –

and equally importantly – there was a clear statement of the difficulties remaining, anticipated future problems, and an outline of how the team proposed to tackle these in the rehabilitation phase.

It was important to find out from the other agencies whether the changes observed in Sandra were replicated in her continued contacts with their professionals. This conference heard firm opinions that this was definitely so. The social services department formally accepted the recommendation that Jeremy return 'home on trial' on the basis of the rehabilitation contract described. The conference also accepted the team's recommendation that no statutory action was necessary in respect of Sandra's unborn baby.

It was also important to recognize that there could be renewed conflict between agencies once Jeremy was returned to Sandra's care. Each professional was asked to state specifically what their continuing roles would be. The Family Centre workers were clear that they would tightly regulate their offer to Sandra of continuing attendance at their Centre on two days a week. All agencies agreed that any significant problems arising would be dealt with by the NSPCC team which would continue to see Sandra and Jeremy for sessions during the period of rehabilitation.

Third family–agency meeting

Immediately following the case-conference the team had arranged for the professionals directly involved with the family to meet with Sandra. The purpose of the meeting was to give Sandra maximum understanding of the conditions attached to Jeremy's return home, and to demonstrate to her that the professional group was united in its approach to her. Each professional gave Sandra a precise and appropriate statement of what they were offering her – as well as what they were *not* offering her. This was of particular importance in this case as originally Sandra had mercilessly exploited professional role confusions and conflicts. All parties stressed to her that she would be responsible for the acceptable care of Jeremy, and that any resumption of her dangerous games with him and manipulative games with the agencies would not be tolerated. To the consultant observing, the atmosphere of this meeting contrasted to a marked extent with the previous one at the beginning of the assessment. It was clear that it was not only

Sandra who had changed. Her mood of increased confidence and competence was mirrored in the presentations of all the other professionals. Sandra had learned a lot and changed significantly; and so had they.

Discussion: Influence of five systems

The family system

Family therapists may be disappointed that in this presentation space has not allowed for a detailed 'systemic' consideration of Sandra's position within her family network. In particular it has not been possible to describe the complex relationship between Sandra and her boyfriend and the influence of his family, or her continuing (and changing) relationship with her own mother.

Not too much may have been lost, however, and readers with experience of disturbed families in any context will have gained a 'feel' of the sorts of dynamics in operation from the brief descriptions given. Sandra's skills at manipulation and 'game playing' were learned early on in a family characterized by chaotic and rapidly changing relationships, concentration on adult needs, and powerfully disturbing mixed messages and double binds. Sandra's adult relationships continued to be affected by these experiences, and with David in particular she continued to express ambivalent and contradictory feelings of wanting both proximity and distance from him. It was precisely such feelings which originally lay behind her bizarre behaviour and relationship with Jeremy. It was on this area that the therapeutic work had focused, and where significant changes had occurred.

Family therapists often feel uncomfortable working in the arena of statutory child care. Work with Sandra represented a very fundamental family therapy, as its main focus was on work with her on finding an agreed definition of what the viable basic family unit was for her. Fundamental change occurred as Sandra moved through the exploration of her ambivalence to a firm definition of her family as including both Jeremy and the new baby.

The therapeutic system

The 'nuts and bolts' of how this system engaged Sandra therapeutically in a tightly structured assessment context have been described. The crucial sessions focused on her *resistance* to the work on offer. In the session with the photographs, emphasis was laid on the importance of the therapist's decision to *explore* the conflict and the power struggle, rather than to try to compromise on differences and thereby avoid conflict.

Central to this therapeutic method is the view that Sandra's behaviour in such incidents reproduced her way of handling similar issues of power and trust in her wider relationships. Although the therapist was the 'here and now' focus at that moment, the real issue was not with him. It was to do with how Sandra experienced control – *being controlled* (e.g. being sexually abused), *controlling* (e.g. her past 'wind up' behaviour with agencies), and being *out of control* (e.g. her previous relationship with Jeremy).

The context of the assessment sessions provided Sandra with firm boundaries, which she seemed never to have experienced before. Her acceptance of the *controlling* context (once that she had tested it and learned that it was firm) gave her the freedom to experiment in a relationship where control – whether controlling or being controlled – was not the predominant feature. Free from having to struggle over power issues, Sandra could set to work in a basic way on her confusion over her identity, looking at her authentic emotional needs and developing an awareness of how she prevented these from being met.

The therapeutic team system

Throughout the narrative, occasional reference has been made to the importance of the therapeutic team as the base for such work. The consultant supports the therapist in the difficult task of remaining 'meta' to the powerful emotions and complicated issues uncovered. The two main dangers for the therapist are *enmesh-ment* with or *detachment* from the family. Enmeshment means that the therapist becomes over-identified with the issues involved, and is affected by the same disabling emotional experiences as the client.

No effective therapists are immune from such pressures, but they will not remain effective for long if they let themselves share the client's experience on a basis of equality. Undoubtedly the client will feel 'understood' and will recognize (and reward) the sensitivity of the therapist; equally undoubtedly, little will change in the client's life. Change will, however, occur in the *therapist's* life – he or she will 'burn out' and rapidly become disenchanted, lethargic, persecuting, or worse. All therapists consciously or unconsciously are seeking to meet their own needs through the therapeutic process. This provides the potential both for creative encounters and considerable damage. 'Helpers' have a responsibility to work therapeutically on their *own* needs, before engaging them with another person's in a professional relationship.

The other danger is that the therapist becomes emotionally detached from the client's experience. This might be reflected in the use of such a rigid programme for sessions – perhaps giving too much attention to a prearranged task – that awareness of the 'here and now' processes within the room is lost. In any interview, whilst prior preparation on the part of the team is important, it is useful to begin by focusing on issues that are significant at that moment. It may be some unfinished business from a previous session, or something new and unexpected. Therapists who rigidly bind themselves to prearranged agendas or unbending hypotheses rapidly lose their potential to create change and create an atmosphere of isolation.

In extreme cases, this can result in the dangerous phenomenon of the therapist becoming persecuting and rejecting, setting the client impossible tasks and failure-reinforcing challenges. Such attitudes may stem from inexperience combined with the therapist's own unrecognized emotional projections, often together with the 'pull' of the particular personality or family to which he or she is most susceptible.

Inter-agency and family–agency systems

Reference throughout the narrative has been made to network meetings as a means of intervention in the inter-agency and family–agency systems when processes are unproductive, repetitive, or 'stuck'. In this case it is possible, even without a detailed description of the professional and political differences and conflicts between the agencies, to gain an impression of how such issues influenced the problem-solving activity of the whole group.

The dynamics operating in the inter-agency system will not be unlike those in operation at the next heated case-conference you attend. In that conference you may begin to pay particular attention to the *processes* operating between the different agencies, and the ways in which these are influencing their behaviour and attitudes, although they are *apparently* focusing totally on the family. You may feel that such processes are unhelpful, as perceptions of the family and services available are adversely affected; or even that they are *dangerous* as children remain at risk because of inter-agency covert agendas.

Add the role of the family under consideration, and remember the phenomenon whereby inter-agency systems often come to reflect, and struggle with the same dynamics as are operating within the family itself. The behaviour of the inter-agency system, particularly as represented by the case-conference, often mirrors the issues being played out within the family. Conflicts in the conference may mirror conflicts between the parents or between the parents and the children, with the professionals taking sides in a battle by proxy (Furniss 1983). Alternatively, a professional may become a scapegoat or may behave delinquently in a conference, mirroring the position of a certain family member; or the entire conference may become afflicted with the dominant mood of the family – for example a *neglecting* case-conference may fail to take action to protect chronically neglected children.

You may take a risk: assume permission, and convene a network meeting to begin to tackle the significant issues other than the behaviour of the family.

Sandra and Jeremy: Outcome

Jeremy returned 'home on trial' to his mother's sole care three weeks before she gave birth to a baby girl. Despite Sandra's continuing ambivalence during the pregnancy, once she had given birth the question of giving up the baby for adoption never arose; they were quickly discharged and went home.

The NSPCC team continued to see the family in accordance with the rehabilitation contract. During the following nine months, nine sessions were held with Sandra and both children. Sandra experienced the wide range of difficulties which any young single mother with two demanding children is liable to encounter. There were times when she was extremely tired, times when she was irritable and depressed, and times when her relationship with Jeremy became more stressful. At all times Sandra responded rationally to the range of stresses she experienced and to her contacts with the agencies directly involved with her. There was no suggestion of any return to the previous pattern of bizarre and threatening behaviour, or of any mechanisms of covert communication. Sandra remained refreshingly honest: when she was fed up she said so; when the children were annoying her with their demands she said so; and when she was happy she showed it. Sandra had become a normal mother with normal problems.

By joint agreement, sessions with the NSPCC team ended, Sandra continuing in a contracted pattern of attendance at the Family Centre. Twelve months after the ending of contact with the NSPCC the decision was taken to recommend to the juvenile court that the care order on Jeremy be revoked. At the time of writing, mother and both children continue to do well and are still receiving minimal but highly professional support from the Family Centre.

Comment has already been made on how powerful family processes may be mirrored in the behaviour and relationships of the agencies involved. Such processes were certainly visible in this case as the professionals responded in the early stages to Sandra's unpredictable mental processes and deliberately manipulative behaviour. Sandra initially fostered an acute collective anxiety in a large group of experienced professional workers. It is not surprising that following the period of assessment all the professionals meeting her again were able to mirror her new levels of confidence and competence. Similarly, the relationships between agencies became smoother and far less polarized than at the time of the initial case-conference. Work with Sandra had many positive spin-offs in the inter-agency system of which she remained quite unaware.

Important changes for Sandra herself resulted from her participation in the assessment work, and these have been consolidated since through her continuing involvement with the Family Centre. Sandra would probably have sabotaged the potential for change if interventions into the family–agency system had not been made at times of 'stuckness'. The contribution of the team was to provide the context and the space for Sandra to do her own work and to make her own changes.

It would be naïve to conclude that all will be well for ever for Sandra both as an individual and as a parent. It is conceivable that she will meet further crises at different life stages. However, it is possible to feel confident that if serious problems recur, Sandra will be able to seek help in an open and uncomplicated way; and that the professionals will hear what she is saying and act appropriately.

Peggy Papp (1984) addressed the undeniable reality that effective therapy is a collaborative effort combining the creativity of the therapist with that of the client:

'a brilliant intervention only becomes brilliant through the brilliant use of it made by other people . . . sometimes clients turn our most mundane interventions into transcendental experiences (these are the ones we write about), whilst at other times they remain totally impervious to our strokes of genius (these are the ones we don't write about) . . . and yet where in the literature is the client ever given credit for the part they play in making the interventions something to write about?'

The NSPCC team expresses its appreciation and acknowledgement to Sandra and the other agencies for their creativity in the work described in this chapter.

CHAPTER 7

Rehabilitation

It is important to set individual cases such as Sandra's within the overall context of cases assessed by the team, and to contrast their results with work reported from other studies.

The very different therapeutic approach, and the disappointing conclusions of the NSPCC 'Battered Child Research Team', were described in Chapter 1. The team utilized an intensive, long-term, nurturing therapeutic programme based on the American model pioneered by Henry Kempe. Results of such treatment were reported from a sample of twenty-five children, of whom twenty had received inflicted injuries, with a high proportion – fourteen – classified as severe. Two of them died from the referral injuries.

During the period of follow-up – more than twenty-one months later – twenty out of the twenty-one available abused children were living with at least one of their natural parents – a rehabilitation rate of 95 per cent (Baher *et al.* 1976).

Lynch and Roberts, researching the outcome of a quite different type of therapeutic provision – residential short-term whole-family treatment in a hospital – reported similar findings on follow-up: 88 per cent of the children in their sample (victims and siblings) were living in a family where at least one natural parent was caring for the child (Lynch and Roberts 1982).

Other studies have reported much lower rates of rehabilitation of abused children. Martin *et al.* (1974) found that 63 per cent of their sample were living with their biological parents at the point of follow-up; and Speight, Bridson, and Cooper (1979) reported a figure of 46 per cent.

These statistics demonstrate considerable variation in the placement of abused children and their siblings. To them we can add some figures of our own. For a sample of twenty-six victims (of both serious and moderate abuse), on follow-up (between eighteen months and four years later), 50 per cent were living with their original families, and 50 per cent were placed in permanent alternative families. When siblings are added, the total number of children was sixty. Follow-up statistics of the whole group revealed that 65 per cent had been returned home, and 45 per cent were permanently separated from their natural parents.

It will be stressed in this chapter that such figures in themselves mean very little. Any discussion about the relative merits of different treatment approaches and outcomes must also consider the *quality of life* of the abused children – wherever they are living. It was in this respect that the conclusions of the Denver House team were so honestly disappointing: despite the relatively high rate of rehabilitation, they had to conclude that the children's quality of life had hardly improved *despite* the extended periods of intensive therapeutic intervention.

Similarly, it is clear from the impressively comprehensive statistical analyses presented in the research of Lynch and Roberts, that the rehabilitation rate at follow-up (88 per cent) did not necessarily indicate that the children were living in stable or appropriate families. When only the abused children in their sample are considered, it appears that only 56 per cent remained in the sole care of their parent(s) throughout the follow-up period. In addition, as with the children dealt with by the Denver House team, there was considerable concern about the quality of life these children were experiencing in their 'rehabilitation'.

In this chapter we will illustrate and discuss the principles which guided our team in its recommendations about the rehabilitation of abused children and their siblings. The importance of maintaining a primary focus on the children's continued physical protection as well as their quality of life is stressed.

Decision-making

It was commented in Chapter 5 that there can be no equation for balancing the pros and cons of each available option for an abused child in care; there are no 'checklists' or computer programs to replace the 'godlike' task of responsible professional judgement. There are rarely any simple and obvious solutions – decisions may often involve a 'balance of negatives' where the principle is to choose the *least detrimental alternative* for the long-term prospects of the child.

Decision-making about the future of abused children in care attracts an intense public focus, and a 'new wave' of second-generation public inquiries have highlighted the fact that tragic errors of professional judgement continue to occur. The fatal child abuse inquiries demonstrate that many local authorities make impulsive decisions to rehabilitate children to their parents following serious abuse, and that such decisions are often based on what was identified by Dingwall as the 'rule of optimism' (Dingwall, Eekelaar, and Murray 1983).

Effective decision-making on the rehabilitation of such children can only safely proceed from a clear assessment model and a firm team base. Workers who operate alone and in isolation, and who feel *themselves* to be at risk from public opinion following any mismanagement of child abuse – fearing that they might be the next to be brought before a public inquiry – are in a poor position to make a compassionate evaluation of whether an abused child should be sent home.

Indicators for rehabilitation

Family issues

Responsibility for the injury

It is essential that the circumstances and transactions of the injury should be understood by the team working with the family and by the family members themselves, and that these dynamics should have changed in a positive way. As in work with sexually abusing families, it is a fundamental premise of change that the perpetrator should become able, through the assessment work, to *take responsibility* for the abuse, and that where appropriate the partner should recognize his or her responsibility for behaviour which involved *collusion* with the perpetrator and *failure to protect* the victim.

An assessment of a case of fatal child abuse showed that the taking of appropriate responsibility is an important indicator of therapeutic potential. For example, a three-year-old boy died from internal injuries following a blow to his head which had recoiled against a solid object. Prior to the child's death acute concern had been expressed about the family by the social agencies, and there had been intense inter-agency conflicts about necessary levels of intervention. The assessment followed the mother's release from prison after a four-year sentence for manslaughter. She had ended her relationship with the previous cohabitee, was almost a year into a new marriage, and was four months pregnant.

The couple were grateful for a structured opportunity to review the tragic events in the mother's history, and she used all the sessions to work therapeutically and sometimes cathartically. It was clear that there had been major changes in her personality over the four years since the child's death. She had matured emotionally (she reported her prison experience as having been beneficial in this respect), took full responsibility for the death of her child, and viewed with horror the situation she had created and allowed to develop around her at that time.

The current marital relationship was of a totally different quality to the previous cohabitation in which she had become dominated by, and identified with, the personality of a charismatically aggressive man. In contrast to her loss of identity at that period in her life (a life during which she had experienced an incredible sequence of significant losses and tragedies), she was now able to project a stable personality of her own. This was reflected in the type of husband she had found – a stable, warm, and accepting man. The team had no difficulty in recommending that the baby be allowed to remain in the care of the couple, on the basis of a care order obtained by parental consent as soon as it was born; the baby would stay at 'home on trial' whilst family sessions continued.

The major involvement of the team in this case occurred during the three-month assessment period. Contact with the family continued through family sessions and home visits during the rehabilitation phase, but in fact the stability of the family was such that their very experienced health visitor was able to resolve any parenting difficulties which arose. It was crucial to the successful outcome of this case (another baby quickly followed), that a clear definition of roles was openly agreed between the NSPCC team and the health visitor (Dale 1984).

In many cases the structure of the assessment provides a secure opportunity for parents to begin to dismantle the barricades of denial and projection which they built up in the early stages following the injury. It allows them the opportunity to review for themselves honestly and, perhaps for the first time, together the spiral of events which culminated in the injury to the child. If the abuse occurred at a time of unusual stress – whether social, emotional, psychiatric, financial, material, or environmental – to what extent have the parents taken responsibility for resolving such difficulties, including seeking and using appropriate services? Do continuing, serious relationship difficulties underlie such stresses, or was the abuse an acute reaction to pressures in an otherwise 'coping' personality?

Spouse relationship

The assessment will have focused in some depth on the relationship between the parents as this is invariably a crucial dynamic behind the abuse of the child. Our experience has been that the spouse relationship – especially through the positive changes which can result from therapeutic work in assessments – holds the key to the potential for rehabilitation of the child following abuse. As parents are enabled to work therapeutically on their own relationship with its dissatisfactions and frustrations, they often quickly come to recognize how they had inappropriately drawn the child into the marital conflict. In Chapter 6, Sandra described such processes succinctly with her comment: 'I get at *him* [baby], to get at *him* [boyfriend].'

The team will carefully explore to what extent such dynamics in operation at the time of the injury have changed, and what further changes are required. Is the child's disturbed behaviour still seen as a deliberately provocative act to split up the parents? Or is such behaviour now more realistically seen as an involuntary response to the background of intense marital tension and violence?

The process whereby children are drawn inappropriately into marital difficulties is a feature of many families which experience a wide range of problems, not only to do with child abuse. Indeed it is equally likely to be a feature of families where children are over-protected to an abnormal degree, when the problem may appear as school refusal or psychosomatic illness. In such cases the behaviour or symptom of the child often serves the purpose of maintaining a pseudo-unity in the parental relationship. Parents whose own relationship is severely strained or extinguished may unite in response to the child who demands attention in such a way.

Family therapists are familiar with situations where the *problem is needed* to keep the family together. When through therapeutic intervention the child's symptoms improve, it is invariably the case that the underlying marital problems become more overt and critical. Often at such a point the parents withdraw themselves and the child from treatment, being unwilling to face the reality and implications of their denied marital dissatisfactions. It is safer for the child to become symptomatic or troublesome again.

Similar processes occur in families where the inappropriate role of the child in the spouse relationship culminated in physical injury to that child. The removal of the child to hospital or foster care provokes a crisis for the parents, and opens up the prospect of change in their relationship.

Parenting relationship

The assessment work is likely to have established a history of parenting difficulties, and these will become more understandable as knowledge is gained about the family and social backgrounds of the parents. Three of the most common factors cited when children are placed on the Child Abuse Register are: 'inability to deal with normal child behaviour', 'inability to respond to maturational needs of the child', and 'unrealistic expectations of the child' (Rochdale NSPCC Child Protection Team Annual Report 1984).

So long as the parents are consistently motivated in favour of the children's return home (i.e. if there is no overt or covert issue of basic ambivalence about the child), prospects for the improvement of parenting capabilities through structured therapeutic sessions are excellent. Rehabilitation is *not* dependent on the solution of all child-management problems – indeed this would be almost impossible for children who are in care and thus subject simultaneously to two different sets of parental influences.

What is necessary is that the parents should have a realistic awareness of the difficulties they are likely to experience when the children return, an understanding of how these difficulties negatively affected their own relationship in the past, and an agreed plan as to how to tackle the difficulties which undoubtedly will recur as the children 'test out' the new experience of their parents taking a shared and consistent stance with them.

The child's view

Seriously injured children tend to be at the younger end of the age scale, whilst children with moderate inflicted injuries span the whole range of childhood. It is important in assessing the prospects for rehabilitation to take into account the child's wishes and feelings. This is no easy task.

In addition to being very young, abused children commonly show signs of poor intellectual development (e.g. delayed and immature speech) and disturbed emotional adjustment. The behaviour of such children is often extremely difficult to interpret – is the toddler who clings to a parent showing signs of attachment by separation anxiety, or is he using a self-protective mechanism of clinging and appealing to a threatening and frighteningly unpredictable figure?

The younger the child, the more the therapist will need non-verbal techniques involving individual play therapy in attempting to gain access to the child's internal world and experience of the outside world. Even with older children to whom it is sometimes tempting to relate therapeutically on a mainly *verbal* level, it is very productive to include sessions which use symbolic techniques with dolls, drawing, and plasticine.

Some older abused children maintain a posture of pseudo-maturity on a verbal level, which may not be unconnected with necessary survival mechanisms adopted in their original families. Symbolic approaches are likely to make contact with a more genuine aspect of the child's experience, and to release important material for further work in therapeutic sessions, and in work with the whole family.

An example of this occurred in work with a sexually abusing family. In individual therapeutic sessions, the victim's favourite fairy-story was explored. This was the story of Rapunzel in which the young girl is locked away from the world in a tower by the witch until she is visited by the handsome prince. In later family sessions the therapists encouraged the victim to tell the story of Rapunzel to her parents. By this point in therapy the father was very receptive to the significance of the story, and commented that

his daughter was talking about the prevous life-style of the family –
shut away and unable to communicate. However, the mother was
very threatened by the allegorical message from her daughter. She
demanded: 'Who locked her away, do you mean me?' Such
communication through metaphor provided a potent base for the
successful family and individual therapy which occurred in this
case (Dale *et al.* 1986).

As part of the team's overall work of assessing the prospect of
rehabilitation, it is important for one therapist to form an
individual relationship with the child, and to choose appropriate
therapeutic techniques to explore with him or her the options for
the future. This relationship can develop to include the essential
task of preparing the child for the move from the foster parents
back to the natural family.

Therapeutic-system issues

The relationship between the therapeutic team and the family is a
crucial feature in the process of rehabilitation. It is a fundamental
part of the team's approach that a recommendation for rehabilitation is only the end of the first stage of assessment. The second
stage involves consideration of whether the family can sustain
consistent and appropriate care for the child through the difficult
times which will inevitably follow. The eventual goal of the
rehabilitation stage of work is the revocation of the care order.

In addition to an assessment of changes in family functioning,
when rehabilitation is being considered it is important to review
the quality of the current relationship between the family and the
team. There must be a basic *viability* within the therapeutic
system, and an agreed commitment to continue to work together
on specified issues and tasks. Usually, positive developments in
the therapeutic relationship will have occurred in parallel to
positive changes in the family.

Trust is an important component of a viable therapeutic
relationship. In work with child-abusing families it is essential for
the reality of 'trust' to be consistently reassessed and tested.
Misconceptions of trust insidiously and quickly become dangerous. The Jasmine Beckford inquiry report commented on how the
social worker in the case was misled into 'trusting' the parents to

an extent described as naïve by the criminal trial judge.

The use of a structured rehabilitation context as described in this chapter provides a powerful means for the team to maintain therapeutic authority and to consistently assess the co-operation of the parents following the return of the child to them.

When the team makes a recommendation that the child should be allowed to go home, it is of vital importance that the parents' reaction to this news should be carefully observed. In most cases in our experience, parents show subdued relief or, sometimes, little reaction at all. It is important to explore the significance of whatever reaction occurs. Many parents report at this stage that they had felt quietly confident for some time that the children would be returned, through their own sensitivity to the emotional tone of recent sessions – which may have included very positive whole-family meetings where they experienced greater self-confidence in their own relationships with their children. Some parents report increased positive 'vibrations' from the therapists despite their intention of maintaining inscrutability!

Less predictable reactions may follow which provide crucial indications for the direction of further therapeutic work in the rehabilitation stage. One mother broke down in tears on hearing the news that her daughter would return home, and it quickly became apparent that she was imagining all the things which might go wrong, especially that the girl would miss the quality of life she had experienced in the foster home.

Occasionally, the parents' reactions may be so strange and out of character that considerable further work needs to be undertaken to determine whether in fact the recommendation was correct. We had experience of a couple of cases where such odd and destructive parental reactions followed that the proposal for rehabilitation had to be withdrawn.

It is our practice to inform families of our recommendation for rehabilitation before discussing it with the other relevant agencies through the case-conference structure. In addition to considering the emotional response of the parents, the team will outline to them the *conditions* under which it is proposed that the children should return 'home on trial'. A *rehabilitation contract* will be drawn up by the team to detail precisely what these conditions will be. This second stage of contracting provides a clear demonstration as to the quality of the relationship between the team and the parents at this crucial point. Clearly, any significant resistance or hostility to points in the contract would need to be carefully explored before the recommendation for rehabilitation can be confirmed.

Team issues

Particular care will need to be taken when the team cannot agree as to whether rehabilitation is feasible or not. In a cohesive and experienced team, although disagreements and alternative hypotheses will have fulfilled an essential function in the various stages of the assessment work, it is unusual for such differences not to have been resolved into a clear agreed view of the future of the children by the end of the work.

Following the detailed and intensive assessment programme, recommendations are therefore almost invariably *obvious* during the final phases. Disagreements at this final stage usually indicate that the team has not kept fully in tune with its own processes, and that splits have occurred – perhaps mirroring splits within the family – which require urgent attention.

Inter-agency issues

Following a recommendation that a child should be returned 'home on trial' and parental agreement to the rehabilitation contract, a child abuse case-conference will be convened. The team is responsible for making recommendations to the social services department through the case-conference that are realistic and are generally in line with good standards of social work practice. This includes the principle that children in care should be rehabilitated to their natural families whenever possible.

During the assessment, the team will have encouraged most other professionals and agencies to withdraw from direct involvement with the family. The inter-agency system again becomes crucial, however, once a proposal for rehabilitation has been made. Some of the relevant issues may be raised overtly in the case-conference, and it is important for the chairman to facilitate constructive discussion of them.

Once rehabilitation has begun, many other agencies will have roles, expectations, and responsibilities in relation to the family which need to be fulfilled. This period can bring up complex inter-agency and professional differences which may threaten the success of the programme. Professionals who have known the family for a long time previously may resist the notion that families can change. Some individuals and agencies may continue to be affected by feelings of guilt or responsibility for previous misinterpretations of the family's behaviour, or for actions which turned out to be inappropriate. For a wide range of reasons, professionals who had previously been involved may be anxious about resuming a role with the family.

On occasions such attitudes may be extreme or particularly intense – a professional may for example adopt an overtly or covertly persecuting attitude towards the family. In such situations there is some possibility of professional sabotage of the rehabilitation proposal, and this must be borne in mind by the team who will pay close attention to the evaluation of inter-agency issues at this stage.

Changes in the family demand that agencies and professionals also change. Some professionals, through many years' involvement with a family – documenting in a journalistic way their recurrent crises without the capacity of the family to resolve their own problems ever developing – have themselves become an essential part of the problem.

Another important area for inter-agency conflict at the point of rehabilitation often emerges when previously involved professionals expect to resume contact so as to 'help' the family through the difficult next phase. Inevitably such 'help' will proceed from a basis of different and contradictory therapeutic models.

This description of such issues clearly indicates the vital need for firm agreement between the various professionals and agencies before a child is returned home as to *exactly* what each person's role is – and is not – going to be. Just as the team has a contract for rehabilitation with the family, it is useful for each other agency with a significant involvement to have a similar specific agreement. As described in Chapter 6 in relation to Sandra, the most effective way of minimizing difficulties in the inter-agency system following rehabilitation is to convene a meeting attended by both the family and the professionals at which roles, offers of help, and expectations can be openly clarified.

Mandate for rehabilitation

The legal basis for sending children subject to care orders 'home on trial' to their parents is stated in Section 21(2) of the Child Care Act, 1980: 'a local authority may allow a child in their care, either for a fixed period or until the local authority otherwise determines, to be under the charge and control of a parent, guardian, relative or friend.' Section 16(4) of the same Act makes it clear that it is an offence for anyone to remove the child from the premises where he or she is required by the local authority to live.

In allowing a child subject to a care order to live with his or her parents the local authority must continue to give 'first consideration to the need to safeguard and promote the welfare of the child'. This legislation empowers the local authority to return children to their parents subject to specific conditions, and to allow such arrangements to continue provided that acceptable standards of parenting are maintained. This provides a powerful mandate for continued therapeutic intervention with the family, as any significant lack of co-operation on the part of the parents, or any decline in care-taking standards, can result in the child again being removed from the home.

Many of the public inquiries into deaths from child abuse have dealt with cases where children who had already been abused were fatally injured after being returned home to their parents whilst subject to care orders. Many of the cases demonstrate two major features of inadequate professional performance: firstly, that children who had already been seriously injured were returned home without an adequate assessment of the family; and secondly, that after their return home the level and type of continued professional involvement were dangerously inappropriate.

Therapeutic control in the rehabilitation stage

Use of contracts

The return of a child 'home on trial' is permitted on the basis of a rehabilitation contract. This specifies the conditions which the family is expected to fulfil. As in the initial assessment contracts described in Chapter 4, many of the points are fairly standard; it is also important to anticipate all contentious issues and include a requirement about them. Such requirements may be tailored to each specific family situation. For example, a contract for a family with a history of unacceptable home conditions and neglect would include a clause stating: 'Following the return of the children, home conditions must be kept at all times at a reasonable standard of cleanliness. The team may wish to make unannounced home visits at any time, and on such visits may wish to see the children's bedrooms.'

Specific clauses were inserted in the rehabilitation contract of the ex-heroin addicts (whose assessment contract was quoted in Chapter 4) to cover the history of chronic non-school attendance as well as the other difficulties:

> 'Following the children's return home, neither parent uses heroin or any other illegal drug. No illegal drugs are allowed into the home, and no known drug users are allowed into the home. If any problems in respect of the use of drugs recur, the parents must discuss this with the NSPCC team immediately. The team continues to reserve the right to request urine samples to be tested if considered necessary. . . .
>
> Both children will attend school on a 100 per cent basis except for genuine reasons. Parents will notify the school *at the time* of such absences. If absences become frequent because of illnesses, parents may be requested to obtain a letter from their doctor confirming the illnesses.'

In other cases specific clauses requiring regular paediatric examinations may be used when impaired development has been a feature of the case.

Rehabilitation contract: Example

It will be remembered that a second contract was used in the case of Sandra described in Chapter 6. Sandra's rehabilitation contract was as follows:

> *Agreement between NSPCC Child Protection Team and Sandra P.*
>
> 1. Jeremy will be returned home to the sole care of Sandra. Sandra lives alone at [address]. David will not be allowed to

live in the home without the prior agreement of the NSPCC team. He may visit to have contact with Jeremy at Sandra's discretion, but is not allowed to take Jeremy out of the home. [The condition that David was not allowed to take Jeremy out of the home was included at Sandra's request.]

2. Sandra understands that when Jeremy returns home he remains on a care order. If there are again any serious concerns about his care or development he could be removed again from home without going back to court.

   The NSPCC team will inform Sandra of anything they are concerned about well in advance of that, so that together we can try to sort out the problem.

3. Sandra agrees to continue attending sessions at the NSPCC Unit when requested, and agrees to discuss any difficulties encountered in caring for Jeremy.

4. Sandra understands that because Jeremy is subject to a care order a member of the team will on occasions visit her home. On such visits they will need to see Jeremy's bedroom.

5. Sandra understands that before any other adult can become part of her household, that it will be necessary for that person to be seen by the NSPCC team for consideration to be given as to how that person's presence might affect the care of Jeremy. [This is an important standard clause. It is vital that unknown adults should not be allowed to move into the same household as children at home on care orders without appropriate checks (e.g. for convictions for violent offences) being made, and an assessment taking place as to that person's likely influence on the child.]

6. The NSPCC team recognizes that all active children suffer accidents and regularly get bruises. This will continue to happen to Jeremy. Sandra understands that on such occasions the team may need to ask how a certain bruise or accident occurred, and if thought necessary obtain a medical opinion.

7. During Sandra's confinement the team will arrange for temporary foster care for Jeremy with Mr and Mrs K. (the previous foster parents).

8. Sandra agrees to co-operate with the Health Visitor, and to attend all necessary clinic appointments for both children.

9. Problems arising in the family following Jeremy's return

home and the birth of the baby will be discussed with you in sessions at the Unit, and we would not expect to have any contact with you between sessions except for genuine emergencies. So long as the care of the children remains satisfactory, it is the intention of the NSPCC team to continue working with you until the point is reached that the care order is no longer required, and an application can be made to the court for it to be revoked.

Signed . . . Sandra
Team members
Date

Home visits

Most rehabilitation contracts contain a statement that un-announced home visits may be made. The value of these cannot be overestimated as they allow the team the opportunity of a different context to test out the impressions formed at continuing office-based sessions. Such impressions can also be matched with the feedback obtained from other professionals, for example the health visitor and family doctor who may have more regular contact with the home.

Often it is useful to make such a visit in the early stages following the child's return home as a demonstration that such contact will occur and to test out parental reaction to it. Home visits in the rehabilitation stage also comply with the principle that all children at home on care orders should be visited – *and seen* – with at least the same frequency as required by law through the Boarding-out Regulations for children in foster homes.

It must be recognized as a fundamental principle of the continued protection of children at home on care orders that they be seen in their homes and that their sleeping arrangements be inspected (which is a legal requirement of the Boarding-out Regulations) on a regular basis. In practice, this should mean a visit at least every two months, or perhaps three months in the case of an older child.

It has been our practice in rehabilitation work to separate the 'inspectoral' function of the home visits from the therapeutic work which continues in office-based sessions. Consequently l ome visits may be very brief, with an early appointment being offered to parents if there is a significant problem they wish to discuss. In this way the whole team maintains an involvement in therapeutic work, rather than the member who happens to make the home visit being drawn away into separate and isolated contact.

Expectations of rehabilitation

The rehabilitation phases defined by the contract provide a clear working structure in which the family are made aware of what is expected of them in terms of appropriate care for the children, what help will be available, and precisely what the role of each professional will be.

A responsible professional decision will have been made, with full inter-agency liaison, before the considered risk is taken of returning a previously abused child to the care of his or her parents. The positive changes in the family will have been noted, and probable difficulties forecast. Appropriate therapeutic help will continue on a regular basis to tackle such problems, and home visits will take place as described.

A major advantage of such organization is that there is no pressure on agencies to operate on the basis of *anxious surveillance* of the family, or to provide intensive levels of supplementary services such as day care, family aides, or nurseries. Patterns of surveillance were typical of many of the cases which featured in the public inquiry reports into fatal injuries during the 1970s. Chapter 2 described how such surveillance is at best ineffective for the protection of children, and at worst actually dangerous.

Similarly, the assessment will have reached the conclusion that the father and mother, given continuing therapeutic help, have the potential to provide safe and appropriate parenting for the child. Otherwise the recommendation for rehabilitation would not have been made. Consequently, children will not be returned home on the *condition* that they attend a day nursery or some other form of day care for the maximum period available, so as to minimize the amount of time they actually spend in the sole care of their parents.

Such a practice, which was highly typical of much child-abuse intervention in the 1970s is quite contradictory – if it is not safe for children to be with their parents between 9 a.m. and 5 p.m. on weekdays, it cannot be considered safe for them to be there at all. Supplementary services such as day nurseries and family centres may be quite appropriately used in the rehabilitation of abused children, so long as they are a specific part of a planned therapeutic programme which is constantly evaluated, and in which the parents are given the primary responsibility for the care of the child.

Therapeutic issues in rehabilitation

Anticipation of future difficulties

It was commented in Chapter 5 that when the team recommends rehabilitation, significant therapeutic work will occur at the final stage of the assessment. It is useful at this stage to have whole-family sessions which anticipate problems which are likely to arise following the child's return home.

The simple technique of *enactment* is especially valuable. Families may be asked to act out or role-play difficulties which are felt to lie ahead; this often triggers powerful emotional responses and movements towards change. In such sessions enactment constitutes a rehearsal of the experience of significantly emotionally charged conflicts between family members in an environment which is both real and contrived. It is a *safe emergency*. The following simple example best illustrates the process.

A ten-year-old boy was to return home to his family. One area of significant difficulty that his parents anticipated was competitiveness and squabbling between him and his younger brother which at times could become quite vicious. The view of the therapists was that the sibling fighting was in itself less significant than the roles and actions that the parents were willing to agree to take to control it appropriately. In a session shortly before rehabilitation, the verbal focus was on another issue, but throughout the two boys were constantly niggling and kicking at each other. The therapists invited them to show how well they could *really* squabble and fight.

As with any paradoxical type of intervention, the boys' reaction was momentarily one of surprise and puzzlement. The therapists reinforced the request. Both boys rose to the challenge and very quickly were fighting for real on the floor. The therapists simply looked at the parents.

One of the family's fundamental problems of parenting was thus re-created in this simple, dramatic way within the therapeutic session. The task for the parents was to test out and rehearse more effective ways of dealing with a situation they had previously dealt with inappropriately. In fact in this case the father found that *he* had to take some action – he could no longer continue to opt out of a controlling role with his stepsons. The mother then began to realize that she would have to accept and support her husband as he developed this role.

Enacting such issues during therapeutic sessions provides a far more potent and rapid learning experience for all participants than would be obtained in a series of sessions spent talking *about* the problem.

The scope of appropriate enactment techniques is limited only by the imagination of the team. Tasks for all age groups can be used. In the work with Sandra, the team once arranged the timing of her session with Jeremy so as to make him miss his afternoon sleep, and consequently be fractious. A tantrum from Jeremy for Sandra to manage in the session was guaranteed.

The child's return home

In most cases we do not favour the *phased* return home of children from foster care. The practice of gradually building up the length of time a child spends back in his own home from a continuing base in the foster home has been common among many practitioners. On occasions this may be quite an extended and complicated process with the child spending some nights in the parents' home, and others in the foster home.

In our view this practice reflects agency anxiety as to whether the decision to return the child home was right; it is not the most effective way of re-establishing the child with his own family. Following a recommendation for rehabilitation, it is vital for appropriate preparation work to be done with the child, the natural family, and the foster family, to enable him or her to return home in one highly significant and well-planned move. This is the clearest way of telling the parents of the confidence which the agencies have in their ability to care appropriately for the child, and of their responsibility to use the continuing therapeutic help to justify this confidence.

Stage of readjustment and consolidation

Children who have been in care following physical abuse from their parents and who then return home, generally respond immediately in one of two ways: they either 'test out' the security of their return *immediately* by various forms of difficult or uncooperative behaviour; or they allow a 'honeymoon period' to expire and *then* test out their parents in exactly the same ways.

At an early stage it is likely that the parents will need to work hard to maintain a response of warm, firm, and consistent handling of the children. The team will schedule the frequency of therapeutic sessions to match the intensity of the task in hand. It may be that some of these sessions do not include the children, but are used to concentrate on tensions which may arise in the marital relationship at such times of stress.

The maintenance of positive changes in the marital relationship is a key factor in successful rehabilitation. In two-parent families it is only from the basis of a mutually satisfactory marital relationship that consistent parenting of the children can be maintained without a regression back to earlier – and manifestly dangerous – patterns by which the children were inappropriately drawn into marital conflict and dissatisfactions.

Extensive work to maintain positive changes in a marital relationship gained during the assessment period was done during the rehabilitation of a child seriously injured in an accident in which her two siblings were killed. The two girls had died in a car driven and deliberately crashed by their father who had driven off telling his wife he intended to kill himself and the three children following an intense marital row. In fact the father was uninjured, and the third child recovered after major surgery. The father was convicted of two offences of manslaughter and sentenced to four years' imprisonment. The mother and the surviving child, Suzanne, remained at home.

The assessment referral was made when a date for possible parole was set, the task being to recommend whether or not Suzanne could be allowed to remain in her father's household when he was released. With the support of the prison authorities, fifteen weekly sessions took place in a private setting within the prison.

Genogram work revealed a history of strong mutual dependence between the spouses, and charted how their relationship had already survived several previous serious crises. This work also demonstrated how the spouse relationship had consistently operated around a series of power struggles in which behaviour on both sides became increasingly dramatic. The fatal incident could be interpreted in this light. In a continuing cycle of provocation and retaliation, the mother had provoked her husband's known pathological jealousy by flirting mildly with a friend. In previous similar incidents he had responded with serious suicide attempts which she had largely ignored. Ultimately, and almost inevitably, the stakes were raised, and the children were brought inappropriately and fatally into this circular marital conflict.

In the assessment work there was a major focus on the 'here and now' relationship between the couple, with the object of making overt these circular processes of 'wind-ups' and retaliation. Work on communication was also important, to decrease the couple's habitual heavy reliance on covert communication. Much concern was felt about the continued inhibition of emotional expression in both parents which had clearly contributed towards their explosiveness. Suzanne's role of 'go-between' for her parents was seen to diminish significantly.

The team felt concern about the father's continued potential for explosiveness, but it was recognized that the couple had worked productively, and could work further, to change the provocative transactions in their relationship which continued to have an aspect of hostile dependency. On the other hand, it was evident that Suzanne's attachment to both parents was firm and consistent, and that she would suffer emotionally from any plan to separate her from them.

It was ultimately recommended that Suzanne be allowed to live with her father following his release, but subject to a care order obtained (by consent) beforehand. The care order had the crucial function of providing a firm mandate for the team to continue work with the family – if necessary over a long period of time. In addition it would lessen the mother's ability to use Suzanne in any recurrence of the 'wind-ups' (in which she used to threaten to leave with the children), because the local authority would have legal control over where Suzanne lived.

Rehabilitation sessions continued on a regular basis for two years following the father's release from prison, and the spouse relationship remained stable, both parents demonstrating considerably increased levels of maturity. An important consequence of this was that both parents became able to help Suzanne grieve appropriately for her lost sisters.

Parental resistance to the team in the rehabilitation stage

It is not uncommon for the parents to make some sign of resistance to continuing contact with the team once the children have been returned home. Such responses require very careful evaluation by the team. They are likely to involve some level of lack of compliance with the contract, failure to attend appointments either with the therapists or another professional perhaps being the most common example.

It is important for the team to demonstrate to the parents at such times that the contract is the basis of the child's placement at home, and that its requirements must be fulfilled. Consequently, a failed appointment, particularly in the initial stages, will elicit the response of a fairly immediate home visit. The child will be seen, and the parents questioned about their non-attendance. *The response of the parents will provide crucial information about the current functioning of the therapeutic system.* To what extent was there a genuine reason for the missed appointment, e.g. a genuine and observable illness for which appropriate treatment was sought? Did they contact, or attempt to contact, the team with a message to explain this? If not, why not? To what extent is there a hostile, sullen, embarrassed, or passive reaction to the home visit? What happened when this was explored and the requirement for attendance at appointments stressed?

The therapists will form an opinion of the significance of the event, and will either feel reassured or more concerned. Either way, another appointment will be given in the near future, to test out further the relationship with the family, and the viability of the conditions of rehabilitation.

During the home visit, important information will be gained about how the family is functioning. Is the mood as open, optimistic, and energetic as it was at the time the child returned, or have there been significant changes? What is the behaviour, mood, and reaction of the child to the familiar figure of the therapist? Is the child subdued and sensitive to the 'crisis', or relaxed, and chattering about pleasant family events?

In cases where the therapists perceive significant resistance, it is important that this be tackled at an early stage in formal sessions. Our experience has been that resistance to the therapists at this point involves a *projection* on the part of the parents of renewed, serious family problems which they wish to keep secret.

Clearly at such times, many parents are concerned that if they are open about the difficulties they may be having with each other or the child, the team will take this as a signal to precipitately remove the child again. The issue of trust in the therapeutic relationship at all times remains a crucial factor.

Trust is best engendered if the therapists remain consistent and predictable, and insist that the conditions agreed for the return of the child are observed. Ultimately, if parents continually fail to keep appointments, and refuse to discuss parenting or marital difficulties which are covert but obvious, and the child's behaviour and emotional adjustment are observed to be deteriorating – the child must be protected by being taken back into care.

In our experience of only a small number of failed rehabilitations, the parents refusal to co-operate with the previously agreed conditions constituted the overt sign of a recurrence of serious marital difficulties or an underlying, masked rejection of the child. We take satisfaction that the children involved in such cases were taken back into care *before* any reinjuries occurred.

More commonly, the recurrence of parental resistance to the therapists at this stage represents an understandable, appropriate, and even ingenious attempt by them to *test out* the reality of external controls after the return of the child. Undoubtedly, some parents do this – perhaps by missing an appointment – to satisfy themselves that the security of the therapeutic context will indeed continue when they encounter a difficult phase of family life.

At other times, parents who rapidly become more confident in the success of the rehabilitation programme may begin to have mixed feelings about continued contact with the team, and feel reluctance and increasing irritation at still being in a dependent relationship. The team invariably regards this as a positive step –

especially when they share the expressed feelings of the parents: 'We don't need to come any more.'

It is appropriate and healthy that families moving from a very controlling relationship during the assessment and early stages of rehabilitation begin to test out the possibilities of independence. It is important for the team to consider whether a move towards greater independence is congruent with their own views of the family.

When this is so, our usual practice is to extend the intervals between appointments – saying that no further therapeutic contact will occur for perhaps three, four, or sometimes six months. In the meantime, feedback liaison will continue with the other agencies (with the family's knowledge), and the brief boarding-out home visits will take place. By the time of the next appointment, if all remains well, then the team will consider whether an application should be made for the revocation of the care order.

Developmental issues: The dilemma of sub-optimal development

It has been stressed that a primary requirement of rehabilitation should be that the child has been assessed as physically safe in the care of his or her parents. In many cases an additional dilemma arises as to what is to be considered 'good enough' parenting following the child's return home. In such cases, concern was often felt about the child's emotional and physical development before the incident which led to the care order. Once in the more secure and more stimulating environment of a foster home, such children often show quite dramatic rates of developmental 'catch-up'. This can be easily documented through checks on growth, speech development, and age-appropriate behaviour.

The dilemma must sometimes be faced of whether to return children to a home where it is felt that they will be physically safe, but that the parents (however well motivated) will clearly not be able to sustain the same level of developmental opportunities for them. In the vast majority of cases the answer is that sub-optimal development has to be accepted so long as the level is adequate in relation to the standards of the particular community. The rehabilitation contract can include clauses whereby the parents agree to use the services of professionals who specialize in child development, such as health visitors, clinical psychologists, and speech therapists.

In cases of children whose development was only considered borderline acceptable before they came into care following an injury, their return home will require real progress in both aspects of parenting – the provision of physical safety and of a sufficiently stimulating home environment. It is our experience that in families where there are combined problems of abuse and neglect of a sufficient degree to result in the children being taken into care despite histories of multi-agency involvement, the prospects for long-term, sustained rehabilitation are poor.

Team issues in rehabilitation

Up to the point of rehabilitation, the family and the team have been working towards the specific goal of a decision about the child's future. This will have been a demanding time, and all concerned will have invested a great deal emotionally. Once there has been an agreement that the child is to be returned, much of the energy and stimulus towards change may be dissipated. In the contract a statement will have been made about expected levels of parenting, and the therapists will want to work to protect and consolidate the changes which the family has made. A dilemma arises as to whether the team should continue to push for further significant changes at this stage, or take a lower profile and leave such changes to the embryonic problem-solving abilities of the parents without significant levels of support from the therapists.

A regular experience of our team in work with families in the rehabilitation stage has been loss of energy – even boredom – regarding continuing contact with families who are coping at an acceptable level whilst continuing to experience 'normal' difficulties. For the team this is a less stimulating and exciting time and the danger of collective lethargy must be guarded against. Alternatively, the team may become distracted by more exciting issues which are developing as other assessments begin with other families.

It is important that rehabilitation cases should not be allowed to 'drift', and the consultant should take responsibility for ensuring that the therapists are always working to clear goals within a defined time-span. If there is no therapeutic work to be done, and the child has been at home for a sufficient period of time to demonstrate the stability of the marital relationship and parenting standards, has the time come to consider revocation of the care order?

Discussion

Many treatment programmes for child-abusing families organize outcome figures to show percentage figures of rehabilitation. At the beginning of this chapter, we quoted some statistics from Baher *et al.* (1976), Lynch and Roberts (1982), and our own sample, contrasting *initial* rehabilitation rates with *sustained* rehabilitation rates. Increasingly we felt that such statistics are meaningless when presented outside a context of the *quality of life* of the child.

It is clear from the reports of the Denver House and Oxford Park Hospital projects that major reservations were felt as to whether many of their 'rehabilitated' children were, at the point of follow-up, living in acceptable circumstances. The Denver House study reported by Baher *et al.* emphasized that even if there was evidence to suggest that the risk of physical injury had diminished in rehabilitation, the question remained in many cases of whether the homes were conducive to the emotional development of the children. They concluded: 'With hindsight, we now feel that in several cases, the child's interests might have been better served if the focus of our intervention had been on helping the parents to accept permanent separation rather than working towards rehabilitation' (Baher *et al.* 1976).

Similarly, the Oxford Park Hospital follow-up study (Lynch and Roberts 1982) provided a detailed description of the quality of life of some of their 'rehabilitated' children; much of it makes unnerving reading. In some cases the child's basic physical safety continued to be in doubt as their descriptions of the follow-up interviews show:

'One eight year old boy had had a temper tantrum that day, according to his parents, and did so practically every day of his life. When asked what he did, the father said that "he screams and bawls". The mother interrupted: "Even before you hit him, he screams terribly," to which the father added: "I say to him he could win an Oscar! I occasionally take the whip to him and miss and he goes screaming dramatically down the corridor and collapses in a heap." . . .

One mother described her six year old son's tantrums and stated: "It's very much like Bertie was and I had Bertie put away for it, but I was younger then." She went on: "I end up smacking their legs, including the baby." . . .

'Another mother with a five year old, whom she had always picked on since birth, stated: "I have just given Ray two strokes of the slipper because he disobeyed me three times." She explained that she had called him three times and he had not replied. Her oldest son then popped his head round the door and showed his mother that she had completely split the slipper in two.'

In addition to such open evidence and talk of continuing violence to the children, the researchers also became aware of continuing intense attitudes of parental rejection:

'Another mother said: "I feel as if he's not my child. I wanted to hurt him so much and he wasn't even naughty! It feels as though I didn't give birth to him." . . .

Occasionally it appeared to be that the abused child continued to be the odd-one-out. For example, a six year old boy was the only child absent from the sitting-room during the interview. It took his parents longer than an hour to notice his absence with: "Where's Simon then?" and he came in very timidly, wringing his hands. He sat for a while quietly observing his siblings at play, only to return to his bedroom to play by himself later on.'

Our view of these descriptions of rehabilitated children is that such standards of care, together with actual and constantly threatened violence, are not acceptable. This would be particularly so if these children had continued to be subject to care orders or supervision orders; and in such situations it was neither safe nor appropriate for them to remain at home with their parents.

Re-injuries

Several studies have pointed to an alarming rate of re-injury of abused children and siblings who have been returned to the care of their parents. In a retrospective study of seventy-eight abused children during a follow-up period of between six and eighteen months, Skinner and Castle (1969) reported a re-injury rate of 60 per cent. Six years later, the Denver House team found from a follow-up of their sample that 54.5 per cent of the twenty-two available abused children had suffered re-injuries. Two of them had received *serious* injuries. In addition 22 per cent of the abused children's siblings had sustained unexplained injuries during the follow-up period.

In contrast, during a five-year period (1981–85) twenty-six families were assessed following fatal, serious, or moderate injuries by the Rochdale NSPCC team along the lines outlined in this book. The total number of children involved (victims and siblings) was sixty. Four of the victims had suffered fatal abuse (although not all of these deaths had occurred in Rochdale). Following assessment, 65 per cent of the children were initially rehabilitated with their families (thirty-nine children). Six children (one original victim and five siblings from three families) were subsequently taken back into care because of renewed concern about serious developmental problems or marital conflict, or because of parental failure to comply with the terms of the rehabilitation contract. Each of the three families where rehabilitation failed had significant histories of neglect as well as physical abuse.

From the twenty-six families there has been a sustained rehabilitation rate of 55 per cent. *There have been no subsequent inflicted injuries to any of the children.*

Resources

The initial assessment period involves an intensive input by a therapeutic team over a period of three or four months. This inevitably is an expensive operation when calculated on a short-term basis. However, in contrast, the rehabilitation phase demands only a relatively low input of professional time, all of which can be planned according to a clear structure.

After the immediate consolidation phase following the return of the child, sessions with the family may quickly become spaced out over intervals of three or four months. Revocation of the care order is likely to occur within two years, often earlier. Social work contact with the family – which may have been minimal for quite some time – ends at this point. Acceptable levels of physical and emotional care and child development are sustained without high levels of 'supporting' services from other agencies, and without extended periods of anxious social work 'surveillance'.

We take a good deal of satisfaction that no child who has returned home following a statutory assessment by our team has suffered any further inflicted injury; and that virtually all of these families live satisfactorily in their communities, without intensive long-term professional involvement.

CHAPTER 8

Permanent separation

A decision to recommend the permanent separation of a child from his or her parents, or the removal of a baby at birth from its mother, is a monumental one, and an onerous task for all those involved. It is difficult to imagine any social issue with such far-reaching consequences, not only for the children and families concerned, but also in respect of the broader moral and political implications. Practitioners wrestle with these dilemmas and attempt to resolve them by reference to such unquantifiable concepts as the 'least detrimental alternative' and the 'best interests of the child'.

A major current influence on British and US social work is the principle of *permanency planning* for children in care. In essence this view insists that children should only be in care for a clearly stated purpose: either to return home within a reasonable length of time to more favourable circumstances; or, if this is not feasible, to be placed as quickly as possible in a permanent substitute family. Our own subscription to this view is based on our accumulated experience of previous work with children who had suffered the peculiarly damaging effects of being allowed to 'drift' through multiple placements in local authority 'care'. It is not surprising that many such children grow up to become the parents in child abuse assessments.

One consequence of permanency planning and the assessment process described in this book is that changes in families are required within a relatively short period of time if children are to be returned home following abuse. Essentially, children are no longer allowed to languish in care hoping that their parents will grow up.

This chapter will describe some of the important features of a sample of twelve families where permanent separation between parents and child(ren) was the outcome of the assessment. A total of twenty-one children were involved, twelve of whom were victims of abuse. Of these, nine had received serious injuries. Nine siblings were involved in the assessments, one of these being a subsequent brother of a fatally injured child.

Characteristics of assessments resulting in permanent separation

Failure to engage in the assessment

After the often long-drawn-out court proceedings the parents face the crucial decision of whether to agree to work with the team in the highly structured assessment. This is a significant moment and, as described in Chapter 4, the team will work hard to promote the engagement of the parents in the work on offer.

Two out of the twelve families failed to sign the assessment contract and work did not progress further. In one case the initial sessions vividly demonstrated a violent incompatibility between the partners who seemed only to have been kept together by the shared activity of fighting a 'common enemy' (the social worker) through the court hearing.

The dramatic behaviour of one couple led to the assessment ending within half an hour. The mother and her boyfriend, who was not the natural father of the child, began a fierce row with each other in response to the first question asked about their relationship. After a while the therapists indicated that they intended to take a break, but before they could leave the room, the boyfriend hurled a chair across the room damaging a door panel. The therapists left, and more damage occurred whilst they were out. On returning, the therapists were unable to obtain an agreement from the couple that there would be no further outbursts of violence.

A few days later, the boyfriend turned up alone for a further appointment stating that his girlfriend had left him but that in any case 'she doesn't care for the fucking kids, they may as well be adopted'. The mother failed to attend the further appointments offered to her. Subsequently the couple reunited but did not challenge the recommendation for permanent separation except through an application for access which was dismissed by the court. Following this, the children were quickly placed for adoption.

The other case contained a clear demonstration of a continuing pattern of serious violence in the family. After care orders were made on their children the parents attended two sessions where the assessment contract was discussed but not signed. The couple were given a third appointment but failed to attend and did not make further contact for three weeks. The mother then arrived alone. She revealed that her husband was missing as he was wanted by the police for questioning following a horrific stabbing incident in a fight.

This led the mother to disclose a lot more information about levels of violence in both her own and her husband's families. The response of the team was to attempt to clarify the mother's commitment to protecting her children within this environment. From this focus came an acknowledgement from her that she would not be able to protect them following her husband's eventual return; she was quite clear that she wanted him back.

The crucial point was eventually reached when she stated to the therapists: 'You wouldn't be able to take the risk [of rehabilitation].' It seemed clear that the *only* way in which she could really protect the children was by stressing to the team that it would not be safe for them to return home.

Assessments rarely begin so dramatically. At the contracting stage, over 95 per cent of families quickly sign the contract, often providing important information as they do so. In this context, the behaviour of those families who do not sign is clearly very significant.

Issues from genogram work

The family backgrounds of parents who physically abuse their own children – and who come to the notice of the professional agencies – invariably reveal many of the factors traditionally associated with child abuse in research studies. Almost all of the parents had suffered deprived and disturbed childhoods, with high levels of violence, alcoholism, and neglect in their families of origin.

Two broad groupings emerged from the family trees of this group of abusing parents. One group comprised parents who came from physically violent families and who were themselves abused as children. For many of these parents violence was almost a way of life, a well-established form of communication, and a primitive sanction for adults and children alike. Mothers were as likely to be physically abused as their children. The second group comprised parents from more 'respectable' families – not openly violent or delinquent – but where as children they experienced a pervasive, undermining *emotional abuse*. Often in such situations the child would be expected to become a 'little mother' to younger siblings or, in effect, to look after a parent. Such children develop passive and compliant personalities as part of a pseudo-maturity which involves missing out crucial childhood developmental experiences. The self-protective response of denial of one's own feelings and *suppression of anger* is learned. The seeds of *explosive anger* are sown.

For parents of both groups, relationships with fathers or father-figures had been experienced as distant or overtly rejecting. In the few cases where a father was recalled with warm and positive feelings, early death had abruptly severed the relationship. Mothers had been mainly experienced as over-controlling and domineering – often with an intense, hostile dependency developing. Serious problems occurred in adolescence, and at the point of leaving home to form adult partnerships. For many of the women, separation from their own mothers remained vital, unresolved issues which still consumed high levels of emotional energy.

These problems were most likely to be represented by continuing anger and hurt at a long-standing rejection by their mother, and for there to be little current contact. Alternatively, other relationships showed high levels of contact, but these were characterized by continuing frustrating hostile dependency and mutual provocation. In addition, several of the mothers gave histories of having been sexually abused within their families as children. Such abuse had not come to the attention of any agencies at the time, and demonstrated the pernicious emotional damage which stems from sexual abuse and its suppression over many years. Many of the parents – of both sexes – had devastating biographies. Often the spouse relationships which they formed would 'fit' together to continue the pathological themes of their childhood families.

Wendy was the last of three children and her mother's pregnancy with her was very difficult. She was a demanding and unsettled young child whom her parents found extremely hard to handle. It became a regular pattern that other people would care for her, and be rather more successful. Wendy developed a close relationship with her maternal grandmother, but could recall with some anger the resentment she felt about the distance of her mother. She remembered spending a lot of time as a young child at her grandmother's in order to be out of the way of her father who was intolerant of children and physically threatening. Two major events occurred in her early adolescence: her grandmother died, and her father began to make intimidating sexual demands on her. Wendy complained to her mother, and the approaches from her father ceased until her mother died when she was aged seventeen. At this point her father again attempted to abuse her sexually, and she left home to avoid him.

After leaving home she began a phase of numerous destructive and violent relationships with men. She was extremely promiscuous and in her casual relationships would invariably be physically abused and sexually exploited by her boyfriends. She gave birth to several children in quick succession, all by different fathers. Social workers were constantly, but somewhat aimlessly, involved as the children were increasingly neglected while Wendy pursued the impulsive search for satisfaction of her own needs. One of the babies suffered a fractured skull and broken arm when it was thrown across the room by a boyfriend. The child was returned to her after that man had left, but he was quickly replaced by an equally violent character. Isolated from her family, Wendy's unsettled life continued and several children were neglected, rejected, and abused as the family passed through a succession of temporary addresses in a number of local authorities. Two children were finally taken into care and adopted, but more quickly followed from the relationship with Malcolm.

Malcolm was the second of five children; his parents had separated when he was aged eight. Malcolm bitterly recalled his mother's cruel, rejecting attitude towards him, and her flamboyant sexual promiscuity. He acknowledged a violent, suppressed anger about his early life. As a young teenager he committed a series of solitary offences, including arson at his school, and was sent to a residential school a long way from home. There he remained a solitary figure, causing no trouble but brooding on his anger. On returning home at the age of sixteen, he was summarily thrown out again, and for the next couple of years he lived off his wits, squatting and stealing.

Certain patterns emerged from the two biographies: Malcolm as a rejected child married a rejecting mother in Wendy. The promiscuity noted in his own mother's behaviour was repeated in Wendy's recent history. There was a picture of Malcolm as a deprived child being rescued by Wendy who in the initial stages of relationships would deny her overwhelming need to be taken care of, but would quickly move back again into a testing-out pattern of behaviour which provoked rejection.

Eventually, all the children in this family were taken into care following a serious inflicted injury in the context of chronic neglect. The spouse relationship provided the additional danger-ous component to the loaded individual background of each parent which clearly contained many of the classic features identified in many research studies. In this family the mother had again become preoccupied with her own overwhelming emotional needs, and neglected the children, disappearing for long periods at all hours. Malcolm suspected that she was continuing to form casual promiscuous relationships, and this fuelled his pre-existing pathological jealousy. Of all the children, Wendy was least interested in her husband's favourite; Malcolm attempted to provide this child with compensatory care, perceiving the child's position as a replication of his own in childhood. Unfortunately the child responded aggressively and uncooperatively to his father's somewhat intense but inconsistent attempts to care for him; Malcolm's explosive anger was ultimately fuelled by his experience of the child rejecting him.

In this case both parents were severely emotionally handicapped by their own childhood experiences of rejection. At any stage of adult life they might have been expected to face difficulties in assuming the role of parent successfully. Not only did their explosively violent personalities put them at serious risk of abusing their children, but in addition frustration was constantly fuelled in their marital relationship as they continued a pattern of mutual provocation based primarily on agendas from early life. Wendy – expecting to be disliked and rejected – would anticipate and provoke such rejection to minimize the hurt. Malcolm – fearing his own violence – would withdraw from all forms of conflict and, increasingly, all forms of contact. The children were inappropriately drawn so far into such destructive marital battles that serious injury seemed inevitable.

This case presents typical examples of parental backgrounds in families where serious child abuse occurs. Spouse relationships are based on unfinished business from highly disturbed childhoods; the devastating, unmet needs of the personalities and distorted, tangled relationships continue to be played out in a dangerously destructive manner.

Spouse relationships

It has been stressed throughout this book that the spouse relationship is crucial in respect of the dynamics of the injury and the associated failure to protect, and also as an area of major therapeutic focus during the assessment. Following serious child abuse, if the spouse relationship is not viable, then neither is the family. The children should not return home.

Several assessments terminated when it became clear that the spouse relationship remained totally unstable, and that the couple were not prepared to allow or utilize a therapeutic focus on it. Sometimes this followed an apparent engagement in the early part of the assessment, and the completion of some useful genogram work. Some couples will work co-operatively, even enthusiastically, on historical work when the focus is on each of them as individuals, but demonstrate the chaos in their relationships when current issues are approached. The impression may quickly be gained by the team that *dangerous marital games* are still being played, with the child used as currency. In the fifth session of one assessment the focus was on the current relationship of the young parents:

JOHN. What do I do now? You hate me.

JULIE. No I don't. . . . Do you like my jumper?

JOHN. You're never going to come back to me. . . . What shall we do?

JULIE. We'll wait and see what their decision is.

This couple's relationship was characterized by immaturity and operated primarily at an adolescent level. The unplanned and subsequently injured baby had brought together two young adults with little sustained interest in being parents at this stage of their lives. This illustrates a process which was central to many of the assessments which culminated in permanent separation: there is either an overt or a covert acceptance from the parents that the child does not have a place in the family, or, as in the case of John and Julie, that they simply are not ready to have a family.

Similar dynamics occur when parents demonstrate their *ambivalence* about a child's place in the family. In such cases the discrepancy between what the parents *say* and what they *do* may be striking, and it is usually productive for the team to test this out at an early stage.

An example of this occurred with a family where the two eldest of six children had been in care for several months. The local authority social worker had tried increasingly hard to motivate the parents to oppose the care proceedings, contact solicitors, maintain access to the children through visits to the foster home, and to work towards rehabilitation. All such efforts would be met by verbal agreement and promises from the parents, but non-compliance.

The case was referred to the NSPCC team, and the parents readily agreed to a contract for assessment which included the requirement that they visit the children regularly. They complained bitterly about the unhelpful nature of their previous social worker. Yet when the parents attended the second session, they had failed to visit the children in the meantime as promised. The team decided to test the hypothesis that the parents' behaviour was directed towards their need for the children *not* to be returned, but in circumstances in which they could project blame on to an external authority and absolve themselves as far as possible from feelings of responsibility and guilt.

The therapists informed the parents that the assessment sessions would not continue until they had maintained a regular pattern of visiting the children twice a week for the next four weeks. The result of this was that one month later, the mother had visited briefly, once. The result was that the parents acknowledged ultimately that they could barely cope with the four children living at home, and that there was no place in the family for the two who had been neglected and injured.

Covert rejection of children may often lie behind parental behaviour which social workers and other professionals experience as very puzzling. Often the professional – blinded by a somewhat sentimental model whereby all parents can be helped to love their children – works harder and harder to provide suffocating amounts of 'help' to that effect. The passive, covertly rejecting parent, who continues to feel misinterpreted by the professional, responds in an increasingly uncompliant, nonsensical and ultimately dangerous way. Professionals should always remain aware of the possibility that the parents' incongruent behaviour is a desperate attempt to communicate a rejection of a child which cannot be put into words.

Similar processes may be involved with parents who generally relate aggressively to professionals and agencies. Such situations are often characterized by protracted and bitter court proceedings during which the parents are in a state of intense conflict with every other party. Proceedings may be diverted from the original concerns by parents who make allegations against the other parties – for instance that their child has been abused by the foster parents while in care.

We are not suggesting by any means that all parents who respond in an angry or aggressive way to the removal of their children are covertly rejecting them. Such attitudes would be an appropriate response to the inappropriate removal of a child. However, our experience indicates a definite process whereby aggressive, hostile, and litigious parental behaviour may manifest and conceal a fundamental rejection of the child. This rejection is later acknowledged by the parents during the course of the assessment.

In three of our cases the behaviour of the parents during the assessment remained so (covertly or overtly) aggressive and uncooperative that the work reached an impasse; lack of trust, in addition to the severity of the family's problems, made rehabilitation impossible. Intense hostility or consistent lack of co-operation with agencies by parents may be functional in provoking the non-return of the child. Such decisions in an atmosphere of hostility and 'battles' allow the parents to consolidate their view of themselves as 'victims' of professional persecution. The projection of blame on to agencies may be the only guilt-relieving (or secret-keeping) way of giving up the rejected child.

The three families in this sample who did not move in the assessment towards a therapeutic 'letting go' of the child, contested the recommendation of the team in court through an application for the care orders to be revoked. In two of these cases the parents' application was not successful; the evidence of the team as to assessment work and specific, serious remaining concerns was sufficient to impress upon the court the danger of returning the children home.

In the third case similar evidence was presented by the team to support their recommendation for permanent separation of a baby who had sustained several fractured ribs at the age of four months. In its wisdom, the court granted the parents' application for revocation of the care order, and the baby immediately returned home to their care. Six months later it was readmitted to hospital with further multiple fractures of the ribs.

Explanation of injuries

It has been stressed in previous chapters that the level of responsibility which the parents are prepared to take in the examination of how they came to inflict an injury on their child is a crucial indicator as to the outcome of the assessment. In three-quarters of the twelve cases resulting in permanent separation the team was unable to elicit an accurate and credible account as to how the injuries occurred. In most of these cases the team was left with a firm feeling that the parents were continuing to collude to keep a significant *secret*.

In such cases a hypothesis develops that the family, or a certain member, has a secret agenda which is just as important or more important than the return of the child. Until this is recognized, the team often feels mystified by family attitudes and behaviour which appear to be inconsistent and uncommitted despite the gravity of the situation. This experience most often occurs with passive–aggressive families who contain enigmatic personalities who lure the therapists into working harder and harder to make sense of them with negligible results. A significant feature of such assessments is that engagement and genogram work may seem to have progressed well; then a crisis occurs when the therapists move on to focus on the dynamics of the injury.

The team was involved in the assessment of a family where a

three-year-old child had died following a sustained and prolonged assault. The post-mortem report detailed extensive bruising on every part of the body in addition to several fractures and ruptured internal organs. The injuries were dated to between seventy-two hours and fourteen days before death. The stepfather pleaded guilty to manslaughter, and the mother to cruelty. Both served prison sentences. Throughout their time in prison their relationship remained intact, and on release they were reunited. The assessment began four years after the death of the child when it was discovered that the mother was five months pregnant.

The presentation of the couple at the beginning of work was notable for the father's obsequious manner, and the mother's passivity. Throughout the early stages, work was characterized by a passive–aggressive resistance, although the genograms vividly illustrated their intensely unsatisfying and frustrating childhood and early adult experiences. The critical point in the assessment came when attention was focused on the injuries to the deceased child. The team was initially taken aback by the extent of the couple's *denial*. The first comment by the stepfather was: 'You must have seen worse cases than this.' The parents took the position of insisting that they had not inflicted any of the injuries described in the post-mortem report. They said that the child had been smacked by them, but not for over two weeks before she died. When pressed to explain the injuries and their plea in court of guilty, the parents implied that they had been intimidated by the police, and spoke darkly about an adult relative who had lived with them in their flat.

It was clear that the couple expected the team to accept a vague allegation about a relative as the basis for an agreement that they had been wrongly convicted. The response of the therapists was that if the parents were now alleging that someone else was responsible for the death of the child, then they should make such a statement to the police. The couple refused to follow this suggestion.

The team was concerned about an incongruent lack of concern on the part of the stepfather as to the implications of failing to provide an adequate explanation of the child's injuries. At times he exuded an attitude of smugness, and at one point he tacitly acknowledged that he considered himself lucky to have avoided a conviction for murder. He certainly did not want any further police or judicial exploration of the case. The team gained a consistent feeling that a powerful secret was being concealed by the couple. They formed the hypothesis that this was to do with a previously unrecognized sexual abuse of the girl before she died. Careful perusal of the post-mortem report with a paediatrician raised the question as to whether the significance of genital injuries described in the report had not been grasped by the police or their advisers. It may have been that such physical indications of sexual abuse had been overshadowed by the extensive nature of the other injuries which led to her death.

The couple related as a highly collusive, defensive, and enmeshed partnership, showing an element of the peculiar phenomenon whereby the personalities of such couples 'merge': individual identity and responsibility become blurred, and the couple act as one. The only hope for change seemed to lie in the mother's fleeting awareness that the possibility existed to emerge from the entanglements of denial, but only if she acted alone. The therapists had an impression that part of her was poised to take the step which would allow her to talk honestly for the first time about the events surrounding her daughter's death. This would have serious implications for the marital relationship, and her husband was noted to be exerting increasingly powerful and subtle pressure on her to maintain the agreed stance, even when its implications for the future of the baby had been pointed out:

MOTHER [*to husband*]. You can say what you like. I can't say anything, you don't let me. I'm trying to come to terms with it.
HUSBAND. Go on then – come to terms with it. I will not lie. I don't hit children.
P.D. [*to mother*]. If father wasn't here, we'd get further with you.
HUSBAND. We have no wish to be separated. [*To mother*] I don't want to put words into your mouth. [*To therapists*] I know she has got her dark secrets. . . . We all have. . . . I've got mine.

At the end of this session the team gave the parents the following message, feeling that the only hope for any positive movement would be for mother to take the step towards working alone:

'[Father] knows it is all over. He is prepared to sacrifice this child because he has a greater secret to keep. [Mother] may or may not know what this secret is. She needs to think about her own position very carefully indeed. She must decide whether her future lies with [father] and his secret, or with continuing what she has started today – looking at what happened to [the child] and coming to terms with it. [Father] has no intention of ever making a start on this. The next appointment is on Friday, and we do not know who will come.'

It was clear from the presentation of the couple at the next session that their collusion and enmeshment had been consolidated during the interval. The mother said: 'After we'd been up here . . . we were under the impression that you thought we should split up. We talked about it . . . and I was upset that he said he would find someone else.'

The major feature of the assessment work with this couple was how little had changed since the time of the child's death. Their relationship remained heavily over-invested, each seeking from the other immediate and constant satisfaction of extensive, unmet needs. The extreme enmeshment remained, and continued throughout the assessment when the mother chose not to follow her fleeting inclination to work with the team alone. Both parents maintained their denial of responsibility for the injuries which caused the child's death, and the stepfather on more than one occasion expressed feelings of anger towards the child for 'getting in the way'.

The recommendation of the team that the baby be removed from the mother at birth was based on the view that the couple remained as dangerous and as disturbed as they had been at the time of the child's death. Twelve months later, the baby was adopted without parental consent when, after hearing evidence from the team, the judge ruled that the parents' consent to the baby's adoption was being unreasonably withheld.

Eighteen months after the adoption hearing, the mother recontacted the team requesting individual therapeutic sessions for herself. She acknowledged that the decision to remove the baby had been correct, and stated that she now wished to work openly to understand how she had come to be involved in the death of her own child.

Some of the personality characteristics and issues within the spouse relationship described in this case are typical of features found in several of the families within the permanent separation group. The issue of individual *identity* (or lack of it) is a crucial one. Some couples present as having a totally enmeshed alliance in which there appears to be little consistent discernible boundary between the two personalities. At the extreme the impression of merged identities is given. There is an almost total mutual dependence, usually with a shared paranoid view of the outside world as hostile and threatening. The mechanics of shared identity may involve a dominant personality controlling a passive one through the force of charisma; or a passive personality adopting through identification the characteristics of the dominant partner.

The passive partners in such relationships often impress in their own right as 'failing to exist' or being existentially dead. They project little identity apart from the contact with the other on whom they depend for self-definition. When such relationships do break up, a similar partner is usually quickly found. Such extreme positions of shared, merged, surrendered, or possessed identity provide the basis of peculiarly dangerous family dynamics.

Significance of injuries

Our experience of the assessment of families where serious child abuse has occurred has led us to the view that the seriousness of the injury is in itself a *crucial* indicator of the level of family disturbance, and consequently of the likelihood of the child returning home. This has not been the conclusion of some other studies. The Denver House team commented that in their cases, the severity of the injury had little relevance to the prognosis (Baher *et al*. 1976). Lynch and Roberts concluded that they found little significance in the degree of injury, commenting that chance plays an important part in how seriously a child is injured when a parent loses control (1982).

We would suggest from our experience that such conclusions should be reviewed. It can be useful, in considering the question: 'Why does child abuse occur?', to take an observation from a slightly different angle. Most parents – whether labelled 'abusers' or not – will recognize (even if they will not admit) that there are times when they feel very angry, even murderous, towards their child. Angry feelings, usually fleeting, are part of the *normal* parenting experience. The crucial question therefore is *not* 'Why do some parents abuse their children?', but 'What *stops most* parents from abusing their children?'

Non-abusing parents have an adequate degree of control over their normal angry feelings which are generally discharged in safe ways. Family dynamics are often crucial – it may be that the father or a grandparent is observant and sensitive to the need to intervene at the appropriate moment and provide a break for the harassed mother who is showing signs of increasing pressure and stress. A range of subtle protective mechanisms exist and operate as part of a normal family routine, relieving pressures which could conceivably become dangerous as parental limits of tolerance are approached.

Momentary loss of control

Many parents who cause injuries to their children do not have such an effective and protective network of family and friends around them. There are fewer, and less efficient, safety-valves, and parents are more dependent on the consistency of their own internal constraints. Even in situations where anger with a child does erupt and a parent loses control, in the majority of cases this will be *momentary*, and control will quickly be regained. Many parents after such an experience will be guilt-stricken and may seek help or reassurance.

Even with a momentary loss of control, the level of violence exhibited will be an important indicator of the level of parental emotional disturbance. There is a significant difference between fingertip bruising on a child who has been grabbed and quickly released and the bruising on a child who has been hurled or fiercely shaken. In assessments an important distinction in cases of momentary loss of control is between minimal violence at a time of unusual stress in an otherwise balanced personality and stable family; and *explosive violence* in a personality which has a deep reservoir of unexpressed, historic hate. Is the child struck as a *child* – for whatever reason – or is he attacked as the *representative* of some other person or situation to whom the stored-up rage is attached?

In situations of pent-up, explosive anger – even when the loss of control is only brief – the degree of injury is likely to be at the severe end of the spectrum. In each instance the role of the partner and extended-family members is often crucial. Parents liable to explosive anger are often passive personalities, and may be caring parents – most of the time – especially when they are in company. Relatives and friends (and professionals) may not be aware of the fear of their own violence which such parents harbour; and may not believe them if they attempt to discuss it.

The parent may increasingly become involved in attempts to convey help-seeking signals and warnings, and the misinterpretation or disqualification of these by family and professionals alike compounds the mounting frustration and tension. When injuries have occurred in such circumstances, spouses and other family members may refuse to believe the significance of what has happened, and may create or support a stance of minimization or even complete denial.

In such families there may appear to be a rigid and generalized disbelief, a refusal to consider or acknowledge the reality and meaning of the violence which has so disastrously erupted. The issue for the extended family is one of extreme sensitivity, as it often touches the bare nerves of long-concealed disturbance in the previous generation. Such anger has to come from somewhere. Ironically and tragically, in such circumstances the violent parent is often left in the position of still not being taken seriously as a person with legitimate needs and real problems: a replay of the original family experience.

Sustained loss of control

Some children are subject to prolonged, sadistic, and almost annihilatory violence. In our experience this may happen when the demands and basic needs of the child – indeed its simple presence – threatens the basis of a highly pathological, enmeshed parental relationship. The attack may be by either or both parents, and is characterized either by mutual encouragement or a joint lack of restraint. The dynamics of failure to protect are predominant, and the role of each partner equally significant. Subsequently there is likely to be a firm collusion between the parents who may insist on an implausible account of how the injuries occurred.

A four-year-old girl was admitted to hospital with extensive burns to both feet in addition to extensive and multiple bruising. The entire sole of both feet, and a number of toes, had second-degree burns which had occurred several days previously. No treatment had been sought, and both feet were badly infected. The explanation of the parents was that the burns must have accidentally occurred whilst the child was being tickled lying on the floor in front of a gas fire.

The examining paediatrician was adamant that this could not possibly be the explanation, and that the child's feet would have had to be forcibly held for several seconds against the gas fire to sustain such extensive burns. The police investigation was unable to influence the parents, separately or together, to provide any further explanation. A relative also supported the parents' account, saying that she had been present during the incident, and that the child had not expressed pain. The police seemed to place great stress on the 'respectability' of this relative. Both parents were charged with failing to seek medical attention for the child, and with assaulting her to cause bruising, but not with any offence in respect of the burns. They were both sent to prison.

In situations like this it is extremely unlikely that the seriousness of the injury is determined by any factors of chance; it is more probably due to a highly dangerous set of personality characteristics and family circumstances. Consequently, a detailed examination of the circumstances of an injury will often provide highly significant information which will strongly influence the outcome of the assessment. It has been our experience that serious inflicted injuries reflect highly disturbed and dangerous family dynamics, and that in most cases the children do not return home.

The value of the assessment in such cases is that it provides the basis for a decision about the future of the child which can be presented in detail at future court hearings; in addition it provides a therapeutic opportunity for the parents to work on understanding their role in the sequence of events. A regular feature of assessments which culminate in a recommendation for permanent separation is that the parents tacitly or overtly acknowledge for the first time a long-standing, underlying rejection of the child which may previously have been carefully masked. The structure and content of the assessment, together with the neutrality of the team, can create an environment which enables parents who previously may have been very hostile to agencies, to relax and honestly review their commitment to the child. In this way, seriously disturbed and dangerous family dynamics may be revealed openly for the first time, and the slow process of understanding and change can begin. When such progress can be maintained, the prospect for future parenting may be good.

Permanent separation by consent

Following from this, a major feature of our assessment work has been the high proportion of cases which have resulted in permanent separation with the consent of the parents. In two-thirds of the families in this sample, the parents agreed that their child should be found a permanent alternative family. In most of these cases our view was that the parents had used the assessment to work therapeutically for the first time on crucial issues such as their explosive violence, or an uncompromising rejection of a specific child.

The case of the girl with severe burns to her feet illustrates this process. A long period of assessment resulted in the team gaining a great deal of information about the emotionally deprived backgrounds of the parents, and how they had come together in an intensely mutually dependent, yet fragile, relationship. The mother spoke of her feelings of rejection of the child from the moment of her birth, and how she could hardly ever bear to look at her or touch her. The father's background included an extremely deprived and violent childhood with an unpredictably aggressive father. As a boy he was mercilessly teased over his physical appearance and poor school performance. Eventually he came into care following conviction for an offence of arson.

The relationship of the couple was described by the team at the time of the assessment as 'the comradeship of isolates'. By the age of four, the child was chronically rejected, and increasingly tormented by cruel parental persecution. It was noted that long before the burns were inflicted the parents were aware of the child's seeming lack of sensitivity to pain, such desensitization being a classic sign of a seriously emotionally deprived child.

The major feature of the assessment – after a great deal of initial resistance and denial – was the step taken by the mother especially to speak for the first time about her incomprehensible rejection of the child. Her husband described how initially when he joined the family he had felt sorry for the child, but when she had failed to respond to his approaches he had increasingly identified himself with his wife's violent handling of her. He acknowledged that the time soon came when he surpassed the child's mother in extremes of punishment.

From this work the couple agreed that the girl should not return to their care, and began to get in touch with feelings of horror at the way they had treated her. They did not, however, even at this stage, explain exactly how the burns were caused. It was only two years later during renewed contact in respect of a new baby that the full story emerged. The baby was allowed to remain in their care subject to a supervision order, and therapeutic work began in earnest. The parents now enjoy a very loving relationship with their new child who is enjoying very good and consistent care.

When children are placed for permanent separation with their parents' consent, the parents can be involved in the necessary planning for the child's future. This may involve meeting the prospective adoptive parents, providing information and contributions to the child's life-story book, photos, video messages, and other significant mementoes. This provides the most therapeutic atmosphere for 'letting go' the child, and allows the final placement and adoption proceedings to occur much more rapidly than when parents contest such plans through every legal avenue available.

Future management

When a child is permanently separated from his or her parents with or without their agreement, it is important for a careful decision to be taken about the siblings in the family. If there are existing siblings, then the team will have included a view of their future within the remit of the assessment, and in cases of serious abuse it is most likely that they will also be the subject of a care or supervision order.

If the outcome of the assessment has been that the abused child cannot return home, but that the parents can be helped to provide appropriate parenting for the siblings, then the team will continue its involvement along the lines described in Chapter 7 on rehabilitation. If all of the children have been placed for separation, it is important that the parents be made aware that further work would need to take place before it could be considered safe for them to have the care of any future children.

Recommendations for permanent separation are always specific to the current situation. We are not in a position – nor would we want to be – of recommending that parents can *never* parent appropriately; only that at the present time they cannot parent *this* child appropriately. Following the permanent separation of children who have been seriously physically abused, parents are always informed of the possibility that any subsequent children may be removed from them at birth. They are invited to recontact the team when they decide they would like to begin thinking about a future family.

Recurrent features of many parents of seriously abused children are that they are young, have disastrous personal histories, are significantly emotionally deprived, and are involved in unstable cohabitations or premature marriages which stemmed from a need to escape a past unsatisfactory and often violent life. Many such parents are trapped into a repetitive cycle of shallow, short-term relationships, in which their constant search for the satisfaction of basic emotional needs meets with constant frustration. Children are conceived carelessly and impulsively, and acquire a role as currency in parental bids for affection, attention, identity, and self-worth.

Such families perpetuate an inter-generational cycle of abuse if appropriate therapeutic help is not provided and appropriate child-protective action taken. For many parents with such backgrounds there is little that any form of therapy can do quickly enough to effect sufficient changes for the child to return home. *The child is the primary client*, and when there is a conflict of interest between the parents' need for time to make great changes, and the child's needs for a secure home and consistent parenting, then the child's needs must come first. The major hope for the parents in such situations is that time will promote maturity, and thus open up the possibility of future parenting of later children.

Therapeutic work with separated children: Preparation for placement

It was observed in the last chapter that our team developed the view that 'success' in work with child-abusing families does not only mean safely returning children to their natural parents; success lies equally in enabling a child to make a smooth transition to a substitute permanent family when it is not possible for him or her to return home. An additional element of 'success' in such cases is reflected in the high rate of agreement by natural parents with the plans being made for the child.

Many social workers in social services departments and voluntary agencies are developing specialist skills in therapeutic work with children in care to prepare them for the highly significant transition to their new families. Tremendous energy and planning go into 'family-finding' projects for children in care, and many children who in the past would probably have spent long periods in residential care are being successfully placed in adoptive homes. Particular success has been achieved in providing permanent homes for 'difficult to place' children – those who are older or have behavioural problems or forms of handicap.

The time invested in direct therapeutic preparatory work with such children in the months prior to placement, and in careful anticipatory and supportive work with the adoptive family, is repaid in a high level of stable placements. Sophisticated and specialized techniques for working with such children involve direct emotional expression, and a great deal of symbolic representation through play materials of crucial events in the child's past life, current emotional tangles (especially continuing attachment to parents who cannot care for him or her), and exploration of anxieties about the future, especially the new family – Will they like me? Will I like them? The British Agencies for Adoption and Fostering (BAAF) is an important resource for practitioners involved in such work, and they have published a number of very useful guides and training packs on direct work with children.[1]

The concept of permanency planning for children in care is now widely accepted as essential on the grounds that all children have the right to a stable and secure family life. It should never be forgotten that the permanent placement of first choice for the child is the natural family, and that all efforts should be made and resources provided to enable parents to resume the care of their children – so long as acceptable levels of physical safety and overall care can be attained within a period of time which does not leave the child 'adrift' in an indeterminate placement.

Lynch and Roberts in their follow-up of their sample of abused children reported a large number who experienced placement breakdowns (both at home and in care), and several cases of

[1] BAAF, 11 Southwark Street, London SE1 1RQ.

multiple placements in care. There are perhaps few more distressing sights than a relatively young child who has been so damaged by repeated placement breakdowns that he can only be contained in an impersonal children's home or, at worst, a hospital. The few specialist residential facilities for such children available in Britain are extremely expensive, and in an era of constraint on public expenditure, far beyond the means of most local authorities.

In addition to coming from severely disturbed families, such children are often the product of a lack of decisive action at an early stage on the part of social workers to recognize their fundamental needs and give them priority over those of their parents.

Of the twenty-one children who did not return to the twelve families described in this chapter, only one was not settled into a stable placement with a permanent alternative family within a short period after the recommendation was made. A recommendation for permanent separation represents the end of a troubled relationship for the parents, but the beginning of a new life for the child.

CHAPTER 9

Professional survival

The approach to cases of child abuse described throughout this book has emphasized the importance of therapeutic teams. It is necessary to address the question of how applicable the work of our team – in its specialist setting – is to the majority of practitioners who work in the mainstream statutory agencies. Is there any significant reason why many of the principles and techniques described and illustrated in this book should not be widely applicable to child-protective work in social services departments?

Experience of Rochdale Social Services Department, and many others where we have provided training, suggests that such large social work agencies do have the ability and enthusiasm to respond to and develop new ways of working, and that significant change is possible. In our training workshops we prefer mixed groups of practitioners and managers, although this does not always happen. When we work with managers alone they respond enthusiastically, but complain that their social workers will never allow change. Of course when we work with groups of practitioners, we hear the same line about their managers.

The organization of social services departments contributes to this polarization of 'them' and 'us'. Although most social workers are based in groupings within their agencies called 'teams', such teams are primarily organizational entities rather than cohesive therapeutic resources. A formal line-management supervisory system will exist to ensure that agency requirements are met. The agency may issue detailed procedural instructions to prescribe the frequency of contact with certain client groups (e.g. families with children on the Child Abuse Register) and a primary task of the worker may be to comply with these and the associated adminis-trative activities.

Supervision may involve a process of counting the number and frequency of client contacts, rather than a review of the effectiveness of the workers' interactions with each family. Such supervision fulfils the agency's requirement for monitoring the workers' activities, keeping a record of events in the family (often for no other purpose than for posterity), and noting the agency's responses. Supervisor and worker have little or no shared source of information, all information being controlled by the worker. Even when such supervision occurs in an open and trusting atmosphere, the workers cannot possibly be aware of all the processes operating between themselves and the families, and the supervisor is unlikely to observe such processes directly.

At worst such models of supervision allow the worker to subvert the process by withholding, filtering, or even inventing information so that supervision may become a stultifying and totally dishonest series of transactions. Not surprisingly, in such an atmosphere, there will be little, if any, positive therapeutic work offered to clients. In many cases families will dominate the social-work relationship, and will lead all transactions. The worker and the agency will operate in a *reactive* way only, and often will mirror the family's behaviour: if the family is 'quiet', the agency will lie low. If the family acts unpredictably, the agency will follow suit.

All individual practitioners working alone with child-abusing families in this sort of context are themselves at risk from the precarious combination of professional responsibility and isolation. Burn-out becomes an almost inevitable consequence. The agency problem is then often consolidated as many burned-out practitioners make the only move available to them and become social-work managers.

Burn-out

'The price of burn out is high. Clients are treated badly, dehumanized and poorly served. Communities are robbed of effective public services. High staff turnover, absenteeism and inefficiency are costs borne by organizations. Workers sacrifice their emotional and physical health.'   (Armstrong 1981: 7–11)

'Burn out involves the loss of concern for the people with whom one is working. In addition to physical exhaustion (and sometimes even illness), burn out is characterized by an emotional exhaustion in which the professional no longer has any positive feelings, sympathy, or respect for clients and patients. A very cynical and dehumanized perception of these people often develops, in which they are labelled in derogatory ways and treated accordingly. As a result of this dehumanizing process these people are viewed as somehow deserving of their problems and are blamed for their own victimization, and thus there is a deterioration in the quality of care service that they receive. . . .

The professional who burns out is unable to cope successfully with the overwhelming stresses of the job, and this failure to cope can be manifested in a number of ways, ranging from impaired performance and absenteeism to various types of personal problems (such as alcohol and drug abuse, marital conflict, and mental illness). People who burn out often quit their jobs or even change professions, while some seek psychiatric treatment for what they believe to be their personal failings.'   (Maslach and Pines 1977: 100–01)

Frudenberger (1977) described the symptoms of burn-out as follows:

'Burn out includes such symptoms as cynicism and negativism and a tendency to be inflexible and almost rigid in thinking, which often leads to a closed mind about change or innovation. The worker may begin to discuss the client in intellectual and jargon terms and thereby distances himself from any emotional involvement. Along with this, a form of paranoia may set in whereby the worker feels that his peers and administration are out to make life more difficult.'   (Frudenberger 1977: 90–1)

Many readers of this book will identify – as do the authors – with such feelings at times in their own professional lives, and will certainly recognize many of these signs in the colleagues around them. What can be done to limit the development of burn-out in practitioners working in such consistently emotionally intense areas as child abuse? What can social work agencies do to help their staff who get into this state?

Therapeutic teams

We have stressed throughout this book that the use of therapeutic teams with child-abusing families fosters a quality of assessment and therapeutic service which is far higher than that which any individual practitioner could achieve and consistently maintain. Of almost equal importance, and linked to one of the fundamental principles of our team – 'Look after yourself' – is the fact that working in such teams offers an effective way of avoiding the onset of burn-out. Individual workers are not left alone to deal with and take responsibility for monumental decisions with high-risk cases.

The intensity of the small-group dynamics which develop in the team stimulates intellectual and therapeutic creativity. Work becomes exciting, a stimulating place to be. Therapeutic teams do not work successfully by chance, nor do they fail by chance. Teams need to allocate time to look after themselves. The team's need to meet the individual emotional needs of its members is of crucial importance, and its success in doing so will – usually covertly – affect its functioning on a variety of levels.

One major advantage of therapeutic teams is that they constitute a small, closed, long-term group, and as such a high degree of openness and personal honesty about individual personalities and relationships can be achieved. Techniques of co-working and consultation, with one-way screens and video-recording facilities, produce an exposure of one's professional and personal self which can initially be intense and threatening. Work with abusing families is exhausting and threatening; seldom immediately and sometimes never rewarding. In this context it is vital for practitioners not to neglect their own needs regarding emotional balance and survival.

Membership of a therapeutic team provides an emotional reservoir for members to draw on, in addition to sources of private support such as their own families or their own use of therapy. Whilst this may filter an important degree of professional stress away from the practitioners' own family and be beneficial for that reason, perhaps more importantly it diminishes the tendency for workers under stress to turn to their clients for covert personal support. Having a firm base in a therapeutic team can go a long way towards helping practitioners to avoid the situation of needing to get more from their client families than the families can get from them.

Relationships within therapeutic teams can become mutually supportive to an extent which is inconceivable within large organizational teams. Recognition of personal and professional stress areas, which lie at the beginning of the transition to burn-out, is possible at an early stage. However, the team is not a *therapeutic group*, and it is vital that this boundary be preserved. It is appropriate that the personal therapy of members should occur in a completely different context. Individuals bring to teams their own biographies, and these include different levels of expertise, experience, confidence, and vulnerability. Conflict, power struggles, and issues of competitiveness within the team will invariably develop, and it is precisely these dynamics, openly faced, which provide the energy which is channelled into creative and effective work with families. Teams which avoid recognition of their own conflicts will increasingly become dissatisfied, frustrated, and ineffective.

Dangers of therapeutic teams

Teams which experience the energy generated within the small cohesive group and which operate consistently in an area of high emotional intensity – the physical and sexual abuse of children – become susceptible to certain developments which can seriously affect the quality and appropriateness of the work which they undertake. At one extreme, the level of energy may extend into innovatory activity which may become dangerously narrow, zealous, and evangelical. The team may rigidly adhere to a therapeutic model which becomes practised to the point of perfection, while losing all awareness that families do not seem to be benefiting from it. The team may respond by developing a theoretical rationale for this and 'perfecting' their model even further, whilst becoming so obsessed with their own processes that the interventions with families only represent the latest strategy in internal team rivalry. The team may enjoy power and influence, become 'hooked' on this, and simply seek more at the expense of the humanity of their therapy.

Management of therapeutic teams

The task for senior management within agencies where therapeutic teams operate is to find a productive balance which enables new styles of working to develop (with all the anxieties and anticipated criticisms which are associated with change), while ultimately regulating behaviour which appears to stray too consistently close to the borderline of professional effectiveness or acceptability. Senior managers have a regulatory function in relation to the team, and this will be expressed through the team leader. The leader requires, and should seek, a clear presentation from senior management of the boundaries of agency tolerance in respect of the tasks to be undertaken and the means to pursue them. The team leader needs to be equally open about what is possible and appropriate in respect of demands on the team, and the directions in which the team as a whole wishes to work and develop.

A stable team which is collectively agreed on important issues can exert considerable influence in respect of permissions, change, and support from senior management. One of the greatest threats to a team's stability stems from a lack of clarity about aims and objectives, together with a lack of openness about disagreements which inevitably occur. Stability stems from clearly defined team boundaries and carefully worked-out areas of responsibility. Effective assessment work with families requires a firm and specifically defined *mandate*; the same is true for therapeutic teams operating within larger agencies. Within social services departments especially, the use of *team contracts* with management can be effective in providing mandates for newly formed therapeutic teams to begin assessment work with families. Such contracts permit the members to carry out a defined task at an agreed time (so that they cannot be recalled to do office duty), and clarify the role of the agency manager which may be to consider the final recommendation of the team.

Team processes

The team may go through a cycle of development whereby, in the early stages, the members are intensely involved in creating a distinctive 'model' and style; this may be a period in which degrees of enmeshment develop. The question of the balance between the individual identities of members as against the identity of the team may arise. The balance for the team as a whole between the rewards which accrue from shared activity, and the continuing needs of members for individual expression, may become a crucial process which they must deal with openly. Teams do not consist of clones (in the second year of our team, our secretary commented that she thought we were clones) and few members are prepared to sacrifice their individuality indefinitely to a somewhat fixed team orthodoxy. It is the exploration of differences which provides the energy for a team to develop creatively.

Another notable process which affects therapeutic teams in their work with families is the experience whereby processes within the team sometimes begin to mirror those within the family. It may be that a family avoids conflict, and that the team becomes drawn into not only avoiding conflict with the family, but avoiding conflict within itself for avoiding conflict with the family. . . . In such circumstances, inevitably, the consultant member of the therapeutic team will have become inappropriately drawn into concentrating on the family dynamics, rather than maintaining a focus on the processes operating between the family and the therapists. A similar situation may arise when conflict within families is unrestrained and quite overt. The therapeutic team may find itself having uncharacteristically prolonged and unresolved disputes, and forming into entrenched positions. Often this can be seen to reflect splits between team members who have become covertly identified with separate 'factions' within the family. The team begins to fight the family's battles for them by proxy.

We have described how in work with a sexually abusing family our own team became subject to a quite powerful process of mirroring the dynamics within the family (Dale *et al.* 1986). It is important to recognize that such mirroring processes are not necessarily disadvantageous or detrimental to effective therapy. So long as the processes are recognized, they can be productively incorporated into the work with the family.

Outside consultation to therapeutic teams

We have stressed throughout this book the potency of outside or 'meta' intervention into the relevant systems which surround child-abusing families. The 'meta' intervention into the dynamics of abusing families is called *therapy*; the meta intervention into the therapeutic system is called *consultation*; and we have described interventions into the inter-agency and family–agency systems through *network meetings*. The same principle applies equally to teams – whether they be the large organizational teams within social services departments, or the small therapeutic team of a few members.

Our own team went through a major development after a couple of years when we began to acknowledge that our energy levels were declining, we were becoming increasingly involved in petty disputes and conflicts, and a clear but previously unacknowledged process was operating whereby individual members preferred to work alone than with team colleagues. Communication was no longer open, and hidden agendas were beginning to thrive. The decision was taken jointly by the team that outside consultation on these difficulties was required; they could not be wholly identified and worked on from within. Having agreed on the necessity of seeking help with this problem (as with families and individuals who seek help, a very significant moment), we found a great many practical reasons to put it off for several months.

A team consultation day with outside consultants ultimately did arrive, and this began the process of significant recovery, re-establishment of energy and commitment, and significant renegotiation of relationships. Since then, further team consultation days have been held – not necessarily at times of crisis, but as a recognition that such intervention is a fundamental part of maintaining existing healthy processes and promoting further growth and creativity. We have used outside consultants with different therapeutic interests reflecting the changes in direction within the team. Our first consultants were strategic family therapists; since then we have used art therapy, and *Gestalt* practitioners.

From our own experience, we would stress that teams who regularly encounter high emotional intensity client groups – and indeed all teams – require outside consultation to their internal processes. This need not necessarily mean paying 'experts', as consultation between teams on a reciprocal basis can be stimulating and effective.

Organizational responsibility for 'looking after' staff

It seems quite obvious that if social work agencies expect their staff to provide consistently high levels of service to families where child abuse has occurred – or may occur – they must provide a working environment for staff which facilitates the development and practice of the necessary skills. Morale of staff is fundamental, and low morale is one of the major hidden consequences of the chronic under-resourcing of public services.

However, it is clear from our training workshops in a large number of local authorities that although many of them suffer from similar conditions of social deprivation and diminishing budgets, social work morale varies considerably between authorities. Clear organizational factors seem to lie behind this variation. This provokes the question: what can organizations do to promote good practice, assist professional development of staff, and prevent burn-out?

One factor may be connected with the stability and rationality of the agency's bureaucracy. Staff morale certainly appears consistently low in local authorities which seem to be constantly reorganizing their internal management and service delivery structures. Another significant issue is simply that of the adequate provision of 'tools of the trade'. To provide good standards of child-protective social work, practitioners require good working conditions, including suitable office interviewing rooms, consistent administrative and secretarial support, and realistic workloads. They require senior managers who are prepared to 'fight to the death' to obtain such basic facilities for them.

Practitioners also require training which extends beyond seeing slides of children with bumps, bruises, and burns; but rather, participatory workshops where skills can be learned and developed, and where individual emotional reactions to the issues of physical and sexual abuse can be explored in a safe and supportive setting.

Social work agencies need to recognize the stressful nature of the job that they call on practitioners to perform, and organize pastoral provision for staff at all levels suffering from stress, in a context which is non-stigmatic and separate from line-management relationships. Where *do* the helpers go for help? Clearly, in many areas there are informal channels for professionals to obtain therapeutic help for themselves, but this is rarely acknowledged within most social work agencies.

It is a sad fact that considerable numbers of professionals of all disciplines – many of whom will read this book – are under acute personal stress whilst attempting to protect children, and do not know where to seek help for themselves. It is difficult to become a client of one's own agency, or of another with which one is in regular professional contact; and many professionals additionally feel a stigma against openly acknowledging their own distress. Burn-out is but a short step away.

Social work and other professional agencies *could* tackle this insidious and common problem by promoting an atmosphere in which stress responses are acceptable among professionals. Pastoral counselling in individual and group settings could then be provided on a reciprocal basis.

In the meantime, once practitioners have got to the end of this book, how can they start off the process of change and promote a more constructive agency environment for work with abusing families? Next time you are sitting in one of those repetitive team meetings with the same old circular processes and hidden agendas, take a risk: stand up and silently begin to sculpt the protagonists into physical representations of their behaviour. Things will never be the same again.

References

Annett, C. (1971) *When the Porcupine Moved in*. London and New York: Franklin Watts.

Armstrong, K. (1981), Burnout. *Caring* 7, 2: 7–11.

Auckland (1975) *Report of the Committee of Inquiry into the Provision of Services to the Family of J.G. Auckland*. London: HMSO.

Baher, E., Hyman, C., Jones, C., Jones, R., Kerr, A., and Mitchell, R. (1976) *At Risk: An Account of the Work of the Battered Child Research Department, NSPCC*. London: Routledge & Kegan Paul.

Barclay Committee (1982) *Social Workers: Their Role and Tasks. The Barclay Report*. London: Bedford Square Press.

Boscolo, L. and Cecchin, G. (1982) Training in Systemic Family Therapy at the Milan Centre. In R. Whiffen and J. Byng-Hall (eds) *Family Therapy Supervision: Recent Developments in Practice*. London: Academic Press.

Bowen, M. (1978) *Family Therapy in Clinical Practice*. New York: Jason Aronson.

Brandon, D. (1976) *Zen in the Art of Helping*. London: Routledge & Kegan Paul.

Burton, L. (1974) *Care of the Child Facing Death*. London: Routledge & Kegan Paul.

Byng-Hall, J. (1973) Family Myths Used as Defence in Conjoint Family Therapy. *British Journal of Medical Psychology* 46: 239–50.

Colwell (1974) *Report of the Committee of Inquiry into the Care and Supervision Provided in Relation to Maria Colwell*. London: HMSO.

Dale, P. (1981) Family Therapy and Incomplete Families. *Journal of Family Therapy* 3: 3–19.

—— (1984) The Verdict Was Manslaughter. *Community Care* 27 September.

—— (1985) Montreal Postscript. *Child Abuse Review* 1, 1.

Dale, P. and Davies, M. (1985) A Model of Intervention in Child Abusing Families: A Wider Systems View. *Child Abuse and Neglect* 9, 4: 16–21.

Dale, P., Davies, M., Morrison, T., Noyes, P., and Roberts, W. (1983) A

Family Therapy Approach to Child Abuse: Countering Resistance. *Journal of Family Therapy* 5: 117–45.

Dale, P., Waters, J., Davies, M., Roberts, W., and Morrison, T. (1986) The Towers of Silence: Creative and Destructive Issues for Therapeutic Teams Dealing with Child Sexual Abuse. *Journal of Family Therapy* 8, 1: 1–33.

DHSS (1984) *Guide for Guardians* ad litem *in the Juvenile Court*. London: DHSS.

Dingwall, R., Eekelaar, J., and Murray, T. (1983) *The Protection of Children: State Intervention and Family Life*. Oxford: Blackwell.

Freud, S. (1916) *Introductory Lectures on Psychoanalysis*. London: The Pelican Freud Library.

Frudenberger, H. (1977) Burn out: Occupational Hazard of the Child Care Worker. *Child Care Quarterly* 6.

Furniss, T. (1983) Mutual Influence and Inter-locking Professional–Family Process in the Treatment of Child Sexual Abuse and Incest. *Child Abuse and Neglect* 7: 207–23.

Gouldner, A. (1954) *Patterns of Industrial Bureaucracy*. Glencoe: Free Press.

Greenland, C. (1980a) Lethal Family Situations – an International Comparison of Deaths from Child Abuse. In E.J. Anthony (ed.) *The Child in his Family, Preventative Child Psychiatry in an Age of Transition*. New York: John Wiley & Sons.

—— (1980b) Psychiatry and the Prediction of Dangerousness. *Journal of Psychiatric Treatment and Evaluation* 2.

Gregg, G.F. (1968) Physician, Child-abuse Reporting Laws, and Injured Child: Psycho-social Anatomy of Childhood Trauma. *Clinical Paediatrics* 7, 12: 720–25.

Haley, J. (1973) *Uncommon Therapy: The Psychiatric Techniques of Milton Erickson*. New York: Norton.

Hamilton, J.R. (1982) A Quick Look at the Problems. In J.R. Hamilton and H. Freeman (eds) *Dangerousness – Psychiatric Assessment and Management*. London: Gaskell (Royal College of Psychiatrists).

Hoffman, L. (1981) *Foundations of Family Therapy*. New York: Basic Books.

Home Office Criminal Statistics. London: HMSO.

Lynch, M. and Roberts, J. (1982) *Consequences of Child Abuse*. London: Academic Press.

Martin, H., Beezley, P., Conway, E., and Kempe, C.H. (1974) The Development of Abused Children. *Advances in Paediatrics* 21: 25–73.

Maslach, C. and Pines, A. (1977) The Burn Out Syndrome in the Day Care Setting. *Child Care Quarterly* 6: 100–13.

Minuchin, S. (1983) Conference – Child Abuse in the Family Context. Institute of Family Therapy (London) Ltd.

Monahan, J. and Cummings, L. (1975) Social Policy Implications of the Inability to Predict Violence. *Journal of Social Issues* 31, 2: 153–64.

Palazzoli, M.S., Boscolo, L., Cecchin, G., and Prata, G. (1980) *Paradox and Counterparadox*. New York: Aronson.

Papp, P. (1984) The Links between Clinical and Artistic Creativity. *The Family Therapy Networker* September–October.

Parton, N. (1979) The Natural History of Child Abuse – A Study in Social Problem Definition. *British Journal of Social Work* 9, 4: 431–51.

Pelletier, K.R. (1977) *Mind as Healer, Mind as Slayer*. New York: Dell Publishing Co.

Pickett, J. and Maton, A. (1977) Protective Casework and Child Abuse – Practice and Problems. In A.W. Franklin (ed.) *The Challenge of Child Abuse*. London: Academic Press.

Reiner, B.S. and Kaufman, I. (1959) *Character Disorders in Parents of Delinquents*. New York: Family Service Association of America.

Resnick, P.J. (1969) Child Murder by Parents – a Psychiatric Review of Filicide. *American Journal of Psychiatry* 126: 325–33.

Rochdale NSPCC Child Protection Team (1984) *Annual Report*.

Roethlisberger, F.J. and Dickson, W.J. (1949) *Management and the Worker*. Harvard: Harvard University Press.

Rosenthal, R. (1966) *Experimenter Effects in Behavioural Research*. New York: Appleton-Century-Crofts.

Scott, P.D. (1973) Parents who Kill their Children. *Medicine, Science and the Law*. 13, 2: 120–26.

Sgroi, S.M. (1982) *Handbook of Clinical Intervention in Child Sexual Abuse*. Lexington: Lexington Books.

Shands, H.L. (1971) *The War with Words – Structure and Transcendence*. The Hague, Mouton.

Skinner, A.E. and Castle, R.L. (1969) *78 Battered Children: A Retrospective Study*. London: NSPCC.

Speed, B., Seligman, P., Kingston, P., and Cade, B. (1982) A Team Approach to Therapy. *Journal of Family Therapy* 4, 3.

Speight, A.N.P., Bridson, J.M., and Cooper, C.E. (1979) Follow up Survey of Cases of Child Abuse Seen at Newcastle General Hospital 1974–1975. *Child Abuse and Neglect* 3: 555–63.

Steele, B.F. and Pollock, C.B. (1968) A Psychiatric Study of Parents who Abuse Infants and Small Children. In R.E. Helfer and C.H. Kempe (eds) *The Battered Child*. Chicago: University of Chicago Press.

Stevens, J.O. (1971) *Awareness: Exploring, Experimenting, Experiencing*. Utah: Real People Press.

Walker, N. (1978) Dangerous People. *International Journal of Law and Psychiatry* 1: 37–50.

Watzlawick, P., Weakland, J., and Fisch, R. (1974) *Change*. New York: Norton.

Name index

Subject index